MW01029170

Stand Out Activity Bank 4 Worksheets

Staci Lyn Sabbagh

Rob Jenkins

THOMSON

HEINLE

Australia • Canada • Mexico • Singapore • United Kingdom • United States

Stand Out Activity Bank Worksheets 4
Sabbagh/Jenkins

Publisher: *James W. Brown*
Sr. Acquisitions Editor: *Sherrise Roehr*
Director of Marketing: *Amy Mabley*
Sr. Marketing Manager: *Donna Lee Kennedy*
Sr. Development Editor: *Ingrid Wisniewska*
Development Editor: *Sarah Barnicle*
Contributing Editor: *Alfred Meyer*
Sr. Print Buyer: *Mary Beth Hennebury*
Cover Designer: *Gina Petti*
Printer: *West Group*

Cover Image: *Diana Ong/SuperStock*

Printed in the United States of America.
1 2 3 4 5   06 05 04 03

For more information contact Heinle, 25 Thomson Place, Boston, MA 02210 USA,
or you can visit our Internet site at http://www.heinle.com

For permission to use material from this text or product contact us:
Tel   1-800-730-2214
Fax   1-800-730-2215
Web   www.thomsonrights.com

ISBN: 1-4130-0633-7

To the Teacher

The *Stand Out Activity Bank 4 Worksheets* are the published version of *Stand Out Activity Bank 4 CD-ROM* included in the back of *Stand Out Lesson Planner 4.* The worksheets provide supplemental vocabulary, lifeskills, grammar, listening, speaking, reading and writing activities for the units and lessons indicated on the worksheets. In *Stand Out Lesson Planner 4,* you will find teaching ideas and detailed descriptions of how to integrate these Activity Bank activities into your lesson plans.

Recordings for the listening activities in the worksheets are available as audio files in *Stand Out Activity Bank 4 CD-ROM.* Audioscripts of these recordings appear as an appendix in *Stand Out Lesson Planner 4.*

CASAS-style answer sheets are included in the back of this book. You may want to reproduce them for use with the Exam View ® Pro *Test Bank CD-ROM.*

Table of Contents

Pre-Unit: Getting to Know You

Worksheet	Lesson	Skill	Description
Pre-Unit, Worksheet 1	1	Life Skill	Worksheet – Meet Your Classmates
Pre-Unit, Worksheet 2	1	Life Skill	Worksheet – Admission Application
Pre-Unit, Worksheet 3	2	Academic Skill	Worksheet – Learning Strategies (bar graph)
Pre-Unit, Worksheet 4	3	Academic Skill	Template – Brainstorming
Pre-Unit, Worksheet 5	3	Academic Skill	Template – Paragraph
Pre-Unit, Worksheet 6	3	Academic Skill	Worksheet – Editing Chart
Pre-Unit, Worksheet 7	4	Academic Skill (vocabulary)	Worksheet – Word Family Practice

Unit 1: Balancing Your Life

Worksheet	Lesson	Skill	Description
Active Task Checklist			
Unit 1, Worksheet 1	1	Grammar	Worksheet –*Used To*
Unit 1, Worksheet 2	2	Life Skill	Worksheet – Goal Practice
Unit 1, Worksheet 3	2	Life Skill	Worksheet – Satoru's Goal Chart
Unit 1, Worksheet 4	2	Life Skill	Worksheet – Goal Chart
Unit 1, Worksheet 5	3	Life Skill	Worksheet – Obstacles and Solutions
Unit 1, Worksheet 6	4	Listening	Worksheet – Listening to Advice
Unit 1, Worksheet 7	4	Life Skill	Worksheet – A Letter of Advice
Unit 1, Worksheet 8	5	Grammar	Worksheet – Adjective Clauses
Unit 1, Worksheet 9	6	Academic (writing)	Worksheet – Parts of a Paragraph
Unit 1, Worksheet 10	7	Life Skill	Worksheet – Time Management
Unit 1, Worksheet 11	7	Academic	Worksheet – Time Management Strategies
Unit 1, Worksheet 12	Project		Worksheet – Our Goal Chart

Unit 2: Personal Finance

Worksheet	Lesson	Skill	Description
Active Task Checklist			
Unit 2, Worksheet 1	1	Life Skill	Worksheet – Budget Practice
Unit 2, Worksheet 2	1	Life Skill	Worksheet – My Budget
Unit 2, Worksheet 3	2	Life Skill	Worksheet – Being a Smart Consumer
Unit 2, Worksheet 4	3	Grammar	Worksheet – Contrary-to-Fact Conditionals
Unit 2, Worksheet 5	4	Life Skill	Worksheet – Credit Card Application
Unit 2, Worksheet 6	4	Life Skill	Worksheet – Credit Card Team Project
Unit 2, Worksheet 7	5	Academic (writing)	Worksheet – Buying a House
Unit 2, Worksheet 8	6	Life Skill	Worksheet – Analyze an Ad
Unit 2, Worksheet 9	7	Listening	Worksheet – Complaints

Unit 3: Buying a Home

Worksheet	Lesson	Skill	Description
Active Task Checklist			
Unit 3, Worksheet 1	1	Life Skill	Worksheet – Homes for Sale
Unit 3, Worksheet 2	2	Grammar	Worksheet – Comparative and Superlative Adjectives
Unit 3, Worksheet 3	2	Grammar	Worksheet – Compare the Homes
Unit 3, Worksheet 4	3	Grammar	Worksheet – Comparative and Superlative Questions
Unit 3, Worksheet 5	4	Grammar	Worksheet – Yes/No Questions
Unit 3, Worksheet 6	4	Grammar	Worksheet – Information Questions
Unit 3, Worksheet 7	5	Life Skill	Worksheet – A Business Letter
Unit 3, Worksheet 8	6	Academic	Worksheet – Housing Bar Graph
Unit 3, Worksheet 9	7	Academic (reading/ vocabulary)	Worksheet – Reading Comprehension & Vocabulary

Unit 4: Community

Worksheet	Lesson	Skill	Description
Active Task Checklist			
Unit 4, Worksheet 1	1	Life Skill	Worksheet – Class Telephone Directory
Unit 4, Worksheet 2	2	Grammar	Worksheet – Embedded Questions
Unit 4, Worksheet 3	3	Life Skill	Worksheet – Making Suggestions
Unit 4, Worksheet 4	4	Academic (reading)	Worksheet – Internet Access at the Library
Unit 4, Worksheet 5	5	Listening	Worksheet – Calling for Directions
Unit 4, Worksheet 6	6	Academic (reading)	Worksheet – Volunteer at the Animal Shelter
Unit 4, Worksheet 7	7	Listening	Worksheet – Visitor's Guide
Unit 4, Worksheet 8	7	Academic (reading)	Worksheet – Read for Information

Unit 5: Health

Worksheet	Lesson	Skill	Description
Active Task Checklist			
Unit 5, Worksheet 1	1	Listening	Worksheet – Healthy vs. Unhealthy
Unit 5, Worksheet 2	1	Academic Skill (bar graph)	Worksheet – My Health Habits
Unit 5, Worksheet 3	2	Grammar	Worksheet – Present Perfect and Present Perfect Continuous
Unit 5, Worksheet 4	3	Grammar	Worksheet – Indirect Speech
Unit 5, Worksheet 5	4	Academic (reading)	Worksheet – Healthy Life HMO
Unit 5, Worksheet 6	5	Life Skill	Worksheet – Nutrition Label Practice
Unit 5, Worksheet 7	5	Life Skill	Worksheet – Nutrition Label Quiz
Unit 5, Worksheet 8	6	Life Skill	Worksheet – Medicine Label Practice
Unit 5, Worksheet 9	7	Academic (writing)	Worksheet – Summary Writing Checklist

Unit 6: Getting Hired

Worksheet	Lesson	Skill	Description
Active Task Checklist			
Unit 6, Worksheet 1	1	Life Skill	Worksheet – Skills and Interests
Unit 6, Worksheet 2	2	Grammar	Worksheet – Adjective Clauses
Unit 6, Worksheet 3	3	Life Skill	Worksheet – Job Search
Unit 6, Worksheet 4	4	Grammar	Worksheet – Past Perfect
Unit 6, Worksheet 5	5	Life Skill	Worksheet – Write a Resume (partner interview)
Unit 6, Worksheet 6	6	Life Skill (writing)	Worksheet – Write a Cover Letter
Unit 6, Worksheet 7	7	Listening	Worksheet – Interviews
Unit 6, Worksheet 8	7	Life Skill (writing)	Worksheet – Thank You Letter

Unit 7: On the Job

Worksheet	Lesson	Skill	Description
Active Task Checklist			
Unit 7, Worksheet 1	1	Life Skill	Worksheet – Appropriate Classroom Behavior
Unit 7, Worksheet 2	2	Grammar	Worksheet – Passive Voice
Unit 7, Worksheet 3	2	Grammar	Worksheet – Active or Passive?
Unit 7, Worksheet 4	3	Listening	Worksheet – Finding a Solution
Unit 7, Worksheet 5	4	Grammar	Worksheet – Tag Questions
Unit 7, Worksheet 6	5	Academic (reading)	Worksheet – Ethical Dilemma
Unit 7, Worksheet 7	6	Life Skill	Worksheet – Asking for a Raise
Unit 7, Worksheet 8	6	Life Skill	Worksheet – Ask for a Raise – It's Your Turn
Unit 7, Worksheet 9	7	Academic (writing)	Worksheet – Writing a Letter Asking for a Raise - Editing Checklist

Unit 8: Civic Responsibility

Worksheet	Lesson	Skill	Description
Active Task Checklist			
Unit 8, Worksheet 1	1	Life Skill	Worksheet – Civic Responsibility
Unit 8, Worksheet 2	2	Life Skill	Worksheet – Driving Safety
Unit 8, Worksheet 3	3	Academic (reading)	Worksheet – Jury Summons Information
Unit 8, Worksheet 4	4	Life Skill	Worksheet – Tax Form Calculations
Unit 8, Worksheet 5	5	Life Skill	Worksheet – Register to Vote
Unit 8, Worksheet 6	5	Academic Skill (writing)	Worksheet – Editing Checklist
Unit 8, Worksheet 7	6	Academic Skill (writing)	Worksheet – Writing a Letter to a Community Official – Editing Checklist
Unit 8, Worksheet 8	7	Grammar	Worksheet – Passive Modals
Unit 8, Worksheet 9	9	Team Project	Sample Ballot

Meet Your Classmates

A. Write three questions you want to ask your classmates.

1. _____

2. _____

3. _____

B. Interview four classmates and write their answers in the table below.

	Question 1	Question 2	Question 3
Name:			
Name:			
Name:			
Name:			

Name: _____

Date: _____

Canyon County College
ADMISSION APPLICATION

YEAR _____   (check one) ___FALL   ___SPRING   ___SUMMER

INSTRUCTIONS: Type or print. Answer every question by filling in appropriate boxes or writing information required. Failure to do so will delay your registration.

1. _____ _____ _____
        Last Name   First Name   Middle Name

2. _____ Mother's Maiden Name	3. Date of Birth ___ / ___ / ___ ___ Mo Day Year Age	4. ___ - ___ - _____ Social Security Number

5. (___) ___-_____ Area Code Telephone Number	6. Place of Birth _____ City, State or Foreign Country	7. Sex (check one) ___Male ___Female

8. CURRENT ADDRESS

_____ _____ _____ _____
Number and Street / Apt #   City   State   Zip

9. WHEN DID YOUR PRESENT STAY IN CALIFORNIA BEGIN?_____ / _____ / _____
                                             Mo   Day   Year

List previous residence if current address is less than 2 years.

_____ / _____ _____ to _____
City   State   Mo/Yr   Mo/Yr

_____ / _____ _____ to _____
City   State   Mo/Yr   Mo/Yr

_____ / _____ _____ to _____
City   State   Mo/Yr   Mo/Yr

10. WHAT IS YOUR EDUCATIONAL GOAL?
(check one only)
___Vocational Certificate
___BA/BS Degree after earning Associate Degree
___Maintain certificate or license (e.g. Nursing, Real
        Estate, Fire, etc.)
___Associate Degree
___Education Development (intellectual, cultural)

___Personal development
___Improve basic skills in English, Reading, or Math
___Formulate career interests, plans and goals
___Complete credit for High School Diploma
___Advance in current career; obtain promotion
___Prepare for a new career
___Undecided on goal

Heinle © 2002
Stand Out 4 Activity Bank

Name: _____

Date: _____

11. WHAT IS THE HIGHEST LEVEL OF EDUCATION (BELOW COLLEGE) YOU HAVE ACHIEVED?
(check one only)

_____ High School Diploma

_____ GED

_____ Certificate of Equivalency

_____ Proficiency Exam

_____ Certificate of Completion

_____ Foreign Diploma

_____ Not H.S. grad and not attending H.S.

12. IS ENGLISH THE LANGUAGE YOU WRITE AND SPEAK MOST FREQUENTLY?

_____ Yes _____ No

13. ETHNIC BACKGROUND (check one only)

_____ Alaskan Native

_____ American Indian

_____ Asian – Chinese

_____ Asian – Japanese

_____ Asian – Korean

_____ Other Asian

_____ Black, Non-Hispanic

_____ Cambodian

_____ Filipino

_____ Hispanic – Central American

_____ Hispanic – Mexican, Mexican-American, Chicano

_____ Hispanic – South American

_____ Other Hispanic

_____ Laotian

_____ Pacific Islander

_____ Vietnamese

_____ White, Non-Hispanic

_____ Other

_____ Decline to state

14. DO YOU WANT INFORMATION REGARDING THE FOLLOWING SERVICES? (check each service desired)

_____ Physical Disabilities

_____ Financial Aid

_____ Tutoring

_____ Child Care

_____ Finding Employment

_____ Veterans Benefits

_____ Communication Disabilities

_____ Learning Disabilities

I certify that the statements made by me are true and complete to the best of my knowledge.

_____   _____

Signature   Date

Learning Strategies

Take a class poll to see how many people use different learning strategies (e.g. watch TV, listen to the radio, read an English newspaper, etc.) Fill in the bar graph.

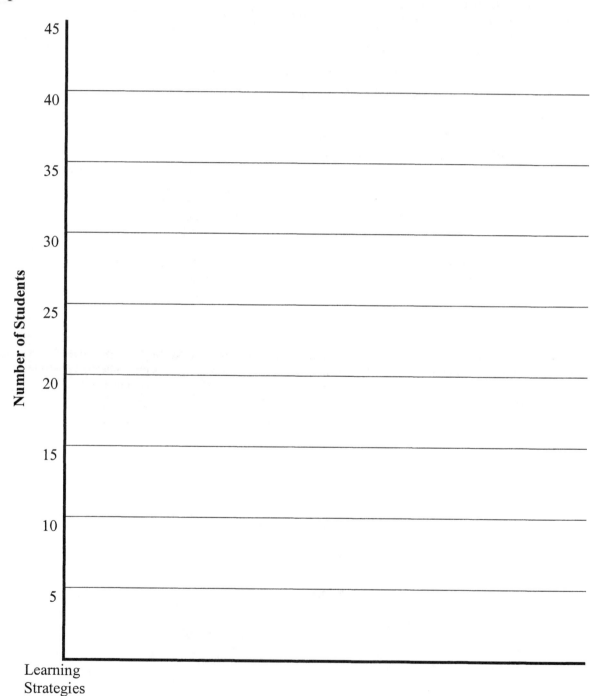

Name: _____
Date: _____

Brainstorming

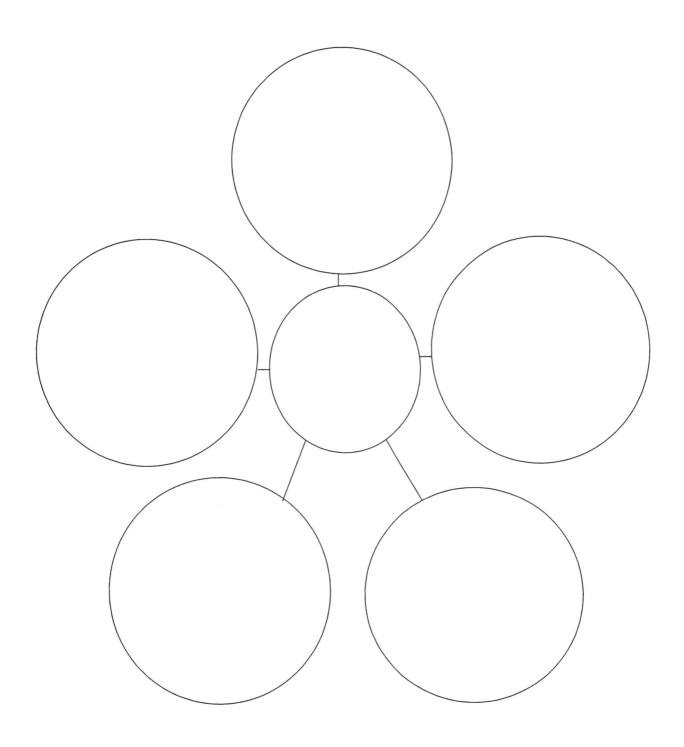

Pre-Unit
Worksheet 5

Name: _____
Date: _____

_____

_____

_____

_____

_____

_____

_____

_____

_____

_____

_____

_____

_____

Name: _____

Date: _____

Editing Chart

Look at your paragraph and find the errors. Write the error in the first column. Then write the correction in the second column. Finally, use the box at the bottom of the page to write the type of error in the third column.

Error	Correction	Type of Error
She are	*She is*	*subject/verb agreement*

capitalization	singular/plural	subject/verb agreement	word choice
punctuation	spelling	verb tense	word order

Name: _____
Date: _____

Word Family Practice

A. Complete the following chart with words in the same word family. (Note: Some words do not have all of the parts of speech.) Use a dictionary to help you.

Noun	Verb	Adjective	Adverb
	strategize		
		agreeable	
			responsively
perfection			
			creatively
	amuse		
question			
		predictable	
belief			
			coincidentally
	imagine		
		presumable	
conclusion			
			comparatively
		confident	
expression			

Name: _____
Date: _____

B. Choose one word family and write a sentence for each part of speech. (For example: agreement, agree, agreeable, agreeably)

noun: _____

_____

_____

verb: _____

_____

_____

adjective: _____

_____

_____

adverb: _____

_____

_____

C. Look at the word families on the previous page and choose one word from four different families. (For example: perfection, amuse, confident, and comparatively) Write a sentence for each word you choose.

noun: _____

_____

_____

verb: _____

_____

_____

adjective: _____

_____

_____

adverb: _____

_____

_____

Unit 1
Active Task Checklist

Name: _____
Date: _____

Unit 1: Active Tasks

1. Complete each Active Task.
2. Write the date you completed the task.
3. Write down the people you spoke to, the information you gathered, or the Internet addresses where you found information.
4. Write down your personal thoughts about the experience.

Lesson	Active Task	Action Date	People I Spoke To	Information I Gathered	Personal Thoughts
2	Use your goal chart to track your goal. Next to each Completion Date, write the Actual Date that you complete each step.				
4	Where can you go to get advice if you have a problem? Make a list of agencies or centers that can offer advice or counseling for different types of problems. Go to the public library or look up counseling agencies on the Internet to find more information.				

Name: _____
Date: _____

Unit 1
Active Task Checklist

Lesson	Active Task	Action Date	People I Spoke To	Information I Gathered	Personal Thoughts
6	Read your paragraph to the person you wrote about or to someone who knows that person.				
7	Go to the library or use the Internet to find tips on time management. Find one tip and tell your classmates.				

Used To

A. Complete each of the following with the correct form of *used to*.

1. They _____ study in the morning but since their work schedules changed, now they study in the evening.

2. Where _____ you _____ live?

3. Sharon _____ want to be an architect, but now she wants to be a graphic designer.

4. How many hours a day _____ you _____ study?

5. Mr. Jacobs lives in Long Beach, but he _____ own a ranch in Montana.

6. Their family never _____ travel.

7. I didn't recognize my old professor because he didn't _____ have a beard.

8. Alice and Quang _____ want four kids, but they've decided to stop at three.

9. Where _____ you _____ study English?

10. Before Mirka retired, she _____ be a teacher.

B. Interview four students in your class, friends, or family and write statements about what they used to do.

1. _____
   _____

2. _____
   _____

3. _____
   _____

4. _____
   _____

C. Make each of the following past tense by using the correct form of *used to*.

1. Leilani wants to be an actress.
Leilani used to want to be an actress. _____

2. The two girls play soccer together.
_____

3. Ms. Tanaka is a teacher.
_____

4. They never do their homework on time.
_____

5. She is thinking about moving out on her own.
_____

6. Arturo is afraid to ask his boss for a raise.
_____

D. Remember that we often use *used to* to contrast something that happened in the past with something that is true today. Rewrite each of the statements above and contrast it with a present-day idea.

1. *Leilani used to want to be an actress, but now she is a flight attendant.* _____

2. _____

_____

3. _____

_____

4. _____

_____

5. _____

_____

6. _____

_____

Goal Practice

A. Gi Hun wants to become a citizen of the United States. Look at each of the steps he must take to reach his goal. Put the steps in the correct order.

_____ Take and pass the citizenship test.

_____ Take an oath to be a citizen of the United States.

_____ Study for the citizenship test.

_____ Become a legal resident of the state.

_____ Pass the citizenship interview.

B. Now complete the Goal Chart below for Gi-Hun. Think of reasonable completion dates for each step.

GOAL:	
Steps	**Completion Date**
Step 1:	
Step 2:	
Step 3:	
Step 4:	
Step 5:	

Unit 1
Worksheet 3

Name: _____
Date: _____

Satoru's Goal Chart

A. Look back on page 4 of your student book and read about Satoru. What is his goal? Write it in the table below.

B. What will Satoru have to do to reach his goal? Brainstorm your ideas below.

Step: _____

Step: _____

Step: _____

Step: _____

Step: _____

C. Now put the steps in the correct order in the Goal Chart below, and write in reasonable completion dates.

GOAL:	
Steps	**Completion Date**
Step 1:	
Step 2:	
Step 3:	
Step 4:	
Step 5:	
Step 6:	

Name: _____
Date: _____

Goal Chart

Use this chart to track your goals. Write in the actual date that you complete each step.

GOAL:		
Steps	Completion Date	Actual Completion Date
Step 1:		
Step 2:		
Step 3:		
Step 4:		
Step 5:		
Step 6:		

GOAL:		
Steps	Completion Date	Actual Completion Date
Step 1:		
Step 2:		
Step 3:		
Step 4:		
Step 5:		
Step 6:		

Obstacles and Solutions

A. Read each obstacle below to your partner. Your partner must come up with a solution for each obstacle.

Example: **You:**   *My car broke down.*
Partner: *You could buy a new car.*
You: *Thanks, that's a good idea!* **or** *I can't do that because I don't have any money.*

1. My son wants to go to college but his grades are bad because he won't do his homework.
2. I want to learn English but all the ESL classes here are full.
3. I need to make more money but my boss won't give me a raise.
4. I want to learn how to use a computer but I don't have enough money to buy one.

B. Now switch. Your partner will read each obstacle below and you must give him or her a solution.

1. My mother is very sick but there are no good doctors in our city.
2. I want to start my own business but don't know the procedures I need to follow here in the United States.
3. My wife wants to work but if she goes back to work, who will take care of our children?
4. My parents are too old to take care of themselves.

C. Now write statements about the advice your partner gave you.

Example: My partner suggested I buy a new car.

1. _____

2. _____

3. _____

4. _____

Listening to Advice

A. You will hear the first part of a conversation where someone is asking for advice. Listen to each conversation and write down the goal and the obstacle or problem. Then brainstorm with a group about possible solutions.

Jenny and her Mom are talking about a problem at work.

Jenny's goal: _____

Jenny's obstacle: _____

Your solution: _____

_____

Mom's advice: _____

_____

Brad is talking to his counselor about a problem with his schedule.

Brad's goal: _____

Brad's obstacle: _____

Your solution: _____

_____

Ms. Jacobs' advice: _____

_____

B. Now listen to the entire conversation and write down the advice that was given.

A Letter of Advice

A. Your friend Maciel has written you a letter asking for advice. Read the letter below.

Dear _____,
(your name)

I'm writing you this letter because you're always such a good listener and you always have such great advice for me. And now I need your advice more than ever! Right now, I'm working as an instructional assistant in an ESL classroom, and I've decided that I want to become a teacher. The problem is I don't have my Bachelor's degree yet so I can't even teach part-time. I need to go back to school to finish my degree but I won't have time with all the hours I'm working. If I work fewer hours, I won't have enough money to pay my bills. But if I keep working the number of hours I have been, I won't have any time to take classes. So you see, I'm in a pickle! What do you think I should do? Please write soon!

Sincerely,

Maciel

B. Write Maciel a letter giving her some advice.

Dear Maciel,

_____

_____

_____

_____

_____

_____

_____

_____

_____

_____

Sincerely,

_____

Adjective Clauses

We use *adjective clauses* to describe people or things. A non-restrictive adjective clause gives extra information which is not necessary to understand the meaning of the sentence. A restrictive adjective clause must be included in the sentence so that it makes sense. Look at the examples below:

Non-restrictive (non-essential) Adjective Clause (requires commas)
Carlos' wife, who works as a nurse in the hospital, is very important to him.   (Carlos' wife is very important to him. *The adjective clause is not necessary.*)   His wife, who was born in Venezuela, is a very special person in his life.   (His wife is a very special person in his life. *The adjective clause is not necessary.*)

Restrictive (essential) Adjective Clause (no commas)
The woman who just waved is Carlos' wife.   (The woman is Carlos' wife. *Without the adjective clause we don't know what woman is being spoken about. Therefore, the adjective clause is necessary.*)   Carlos' wife is the woman who took care of me when I was sick.   (Carlos' wife is the woman. *Without the adjective clause we don't know what woman is being spoken about. Therefore, the adjective clause is necessary.*)

A. Read each of the sentences below and underline the adjective clause. Then decide if the adjective clause is restrictive or non-restrictive. Add commas to the non-restrictive adjective clauses. The first one has been done for you.

1. Heidi's grandmother, who came from Sweden, lives with Heidi's uncle. non-restrictive
2. Minh's grandchild is the boy who won the bike race. _____
3. The girl who has the eyebrow ring is my sister. _____
4. Bita doesn't know what she'd do without her brother who always makes sure she is OK. _____
5. Bob is the person who called me late last night. _____
6. Sandra who loves taking care of children is going to help us with babysitting. _____
7. Minh looks forward to sitting and talking with his grandchildren who are growing up to be wonderful young adults. _____
8. Erin is the woman who cuts my hair. _____
9. Heidi loves her grandmother who has raised her since her parents died. _____
10. Kids who spend a lot of time learning from their parents grow up to responsible young adults. _____

B.   Complete each of the following sentences by choosing a description from the box and changing it into an adjective clause, using *who*.

braids her hair, cooks her meals, and tucks her into bed at night
bring him such joy
~~calls her every day~~
never forget about their old grandmother
raised her when her mom and dad died
stops by to see how she's doing

1. Bita would be lost without her brother, <u>who calls her every day</u>.
2. Heidi loves her grandmother, _____
_____.
3. Eric's grandchildren, _____,
will be going to college one day.
4. Bita's brother, _____,
is very special to her.
5. Heidi's grandmother, _____,
is the most important person to her.
6. Eric adores his grandchildren, _____.

C. Now think of the most important people in your life. Write sentences that give reasons for their importance using adjective clauses.

Person: _____
Sentence: _____
_____

Person: _____
Sentence: _____
_____

Person: _____
Sentence: _____
_____

Person: _____
Sentence: _____
_____

Parts of a Paragraph

A. Label each of the sentences below with *topic*, *support*, or *conclusion*. Remember, in a paragraph there is only one topic and one conclusion sentence, but more than one support sentence.

_____ We always had a roof over our head and food on the table because she was dedicated to her family. ___

_____ No matter how far apart we are, my mother is always with me. ___

_____ She showed me by example how to treat others with kindness and myself with respect. ___

_____ Whenever I had a problem she was always there for me, listening and giving good advice. ___

_____ She taught me how to be a good person. ___

_____ The most important person in my life is my mother because she raised me for 21 years. ___

B. Now decide what order the sentences should go in and put a number after each sentence.

C. Write the sentences in the correct order. Use transitions (first, second, etc.) to connect the support sentences.

_____

_____

_____

_____

_____

_____

_____

_____

_____

_____

Time Management

A. Imagine you are writing an essay on time management. Complete the outline below with ideas you remember from your book and add some of your own.

I. Finding time to study is very important.
    A. Time management strategies can help you manage your time.
    B. _____

II. Keep a schedule.
    A. _____
    B. _____
    C. Check off things that have been completed.

III. _____
    A. Make a "To Do" list.
    B. _____
       1. The A list of tasks is what you need to do today.
       2. _____
       3. _____

IV. Combine two or more tasks and do them at the same time
    A._____
    B. _____

V. Good health is important.
    A. Allow time for rest and exercise.
    B. _____
    C._____
    D. Be positive about your achievements.

B. Discuss the following questions with a partner.

1. What time management strategies do you currently use?
2. What problems do you have with time management?
3. How could you add more time to your day?
4. What are some things you learned today that you would like to use in your life?

Time Management Strategies

Time Management	
Strategies I Use	New Strategies I Will Start Using

Team Member Names: _____
Date: _____

Our Goal Chart

GOAL #1:

Steps	Completion Date	Actual Completion Date
Step 1:		
Step 2:		
Step 3:		
Step 4:		
Step 5:		
Step 6:		
Step 7:		
Step 8:		

Team Member Names: _____
                    Date: _____

Obstacles	Solutions

Time Management Strategies

Heinle © 2002
Stand Out 4 Activity Bank

Team Member Names: _____

Date: _____

Our Goal Chart

GOAL #2:

Steps	Completion Date	Actual Completion Date
Step 1:		
Step 2:		
Step 3:		
Step 4:		
Step 5:		
Step 6:		
Step 7:		
Step 8:		

Unit 1
Worksheet 12

Team Member Names: _____
Date: _____

Obstacles	Solutions

Time Management Strategies

Heinle © 2002
Stand Out 4 Activity Bank

Unit 1
Worksheet 12

Our Goal Chart

Team Member Names: _____
Date: _____

GOAL #3:

Steps	Completion Date	Actual Completion Date
Step 1:		
Step 2:		
Step 3:		
Step 4:		
Step 5:		
Step 6:		
Step 7:		
Step 8:		

Heinle © 2002
Stand Out 4 Activity Bank

Unit 1
Worksheet 12

Team Member Names: _____
Date: _____

Obstacles	Solutions

Time Management Strategies

Unit 2: Active Tasks

1. Complete each Active Task.
2. Write the date you completed the task.
3. Write down the people you spoke to, the information you gathered, or the Internet addresses where you found information
4. Write down your personal thoughts about the experience.

Lesson	Active Task	Action Date	People I Spoke To	Information I Gathered	Personal Thoughts
2	Go to the library for a book or magazine or find a web site that gives advice to consumers before they buy.				
4	Find a real credit card application and fill it out. (Don't send it in unless you really want the card!)				
6	Look at some digital camera ads in the newspaper or on the Internet. How do they compare to the ads in your book?				

Name: _____
Date: _____

Budget Practice

The Lindgrens are a family of four: mother, father and two kids. They also have two dogs. Look at their monthly budget below. Calculate the *Difference* and the *Totals*.

Month: February

Monthly Expenses	Budgeted Amount	Actual Amount Spent	Difference
Auto			
Car Payment	$278	$278	
Insurance	$72.39	$72.39	
Gas	$60	$62.35	
Maintenance	$100	$0	
Housing			
House Payment	$865	$865	
Utilities	$122	$110.75	
Phone (home, cell)	$150	$230	
Food			
Groceries	$350	$345	
Eating Out	$200	$400	
Dogs			
Food	$50	$49.52	
Medical/Grooming	$70	$58.24	
Clothing	$300	$573.97	
Entertainment	$200	$159.42	
Medical	$100	$0	
TOTAL			

1. Where did the Lindgrens spend too much money?

_____

2. Where did the Lingrens budget money but not spend it?

_____

3. What suggestions would you give the Lindgrens for next month? _____

_____

_____

_____

Heinle © 2002
Stand Out 4 Activity Bank

Name: _____
Date: _____

My Budget

Month: _____

Monthly Expenses	Budgeted Amount	Actual Amount Spent	Difference
TOTAL			

Suggestions for next month: _____
_____
_____
_____
_____

1. Write down all of your *monthly expenses*.

2. Write down how much you should allow for each expense (*Budgeted Amount*).

3. Save all your receipts for one month and then add up the totals for each expense. Write the totals in the *Actual Amount Spent* column.

4. Calculate the *difference* between what you budgeted and what you spent.

5. Make some suggestions for how to budget your money differently next month.

Name: _____

Date: _____

Being a Smart Consumer

A. Your friend missed class today and has many questions about what you learned. Answer each question in your words as if you were talking to your friend.

1. Why do I have to *budget* before I shop?

_____

_____

_____

2. Why is it important to *read sale ads carefully*?

_____

_____

_____

3. Why should I *look for price-matching policies*?

_____

_____

_____

4. What does *shop around* mean?

_____

_____

_____

5. Why should I *carefully consider bargain offers*? Isn't a bargain a bargain?

_____

_____

_____

6. Why do I have to *ask about refund and return policies for sale items*?

_____

_____

_____

7. Should I *ask about warranties*?

_____

_____

_____

8. I don't have a computer. Is it important for me to *go online*?

_____

_____

_____

B. With a partner, practice asking and answering the questions above.

Contrary-to-Fact Conditionals

A. Complete each of the following statements.

1. If I had a million dollars, _____.

2. _____, he would open his own restaurant.

3. If she lived in a mansion, _____.

4. _____, I wouldn't study English.

5. If I were the boss of the company, _____.

6. _____, they would never go anywhere.

7. _____, she would buy a brand new wardrobe every season.

8. If their family had a personal chef, _____.

B. If you could live anywhere in the world, where would you live and why? Write a paragraph. Remember to give it a title.

_____

_____

_____

_____

_____

_____

_____

_____

_____

_____

_____

Name: _____
Date: _____

Credit One
Credit Card Application

Personal Information _____

Title (Optional)   Mr __   Mrs __   Ms __   Dr __
First Name _____ MI ___
Last Name_____
Date of Birth ___/___/___ (mm/dd/yy)
Social Security # ____-___-_____

Home Address _____Apt/Suite#_____
City _____ State ____ Zip _____
Home Phone (____) ____-_____
Time at Home Address _____ years and _____months
Do you Own? __   Rent? __
Monthly Rent or Mortgage Amount $_____.00

Financial Information _____

Yearly Personal Income $_____.00
Income Sources _____ (write all that apply)
Do you have a (check all that apply) Checking Account? __   Savings Account? __

Employer Information _____

Company Name _____
Street Address _____Floor/Suite#_____
City _____ State ____ Zip _____
Business Phone (____) ____-_____
Time at This Company: _____ years and _____months

I certify that all of the above information is true.

_____   _____
Applicant's Signature   Date

Name:
Date _____

Credit Card Team Project

Imagine that you work at a bank that has decided to offer a new credit card to its customers. Your financial team must come up with all the particulars for the card and present it to your boss. Then your boss will choose which card the bank will use.

A. Form a team with 4 or 5 people. With your team, fill out the table below.

Name of Card	
Annual Fee	
Annual Percentage Rate (APR)	
Introductory Rate	
Grace Period	
Late Fees	
Over Credit Limit Fee	
Cash Advance Fee	
Cash Advance Limit	
Cash Advance Interest Rate	
Benefits	

B. Present the information to your boss (your teacher ☺).

Unit 2
Worksheet 6

C. Listen carefully as each financial team presents its credit card. Fill in the information below.

	Team 1	Team 2	Team 3	Team 4	Team 5	Team 6	Team 7	Team 8
Name of Card								
Annual Fee								
Annual Percentage Rate (APR)								
Introductory Rate								
Grace Period								
Late Fees								
Over Credit Limit Fee								
Cash Advance Fee								
Cash Advance Limit								
Cash Advance Interest Rate								
Benefits								

D. If you were a consumer, which card would you want to apply for? _____
Why? _____

Name: _____
Date: _____

Buying a House

A. Read each of the statements below and circle the vocabulary word or phrase that best describes it.

1. *"We can probably afford to buy something between $200,000 and $220,000."*
a. deposit   b. purchase price   c. price range   d. mortgage

2. *"After they look at all our financial paperwork, they'll tell us how much the bank will loan us."*
a. down payment   b. mortgage   c. purchase price   d. deposit

3. *"How much do we have to put down?"*
a. credit check   b. get approved for a loan   c. price range   d. down payment

4. *"The seller was asking $210,000 but we got it for $200,000."*
a. purchase price   b. credit check   c. mortgage   d. afford

B. Imagine you are going to buy a house. Put the following steps you need to take in the correct order (1-6).

____ Determine how much you can afford to spend on a house.

____ Gather all the necessary financial paperwork: social security number, tax statements from the past two years, two of your most recent pay stubs, the most recent statements from all your bank accounts, your most recent credit card statements, and statements from any other loans that you have.

____ Get approved for a loan of that amount.

____ Make an offer on the house you want.

____ Ask yourself three questions: Do you have money set aside for a down payment? Do you have enough money each month to make a loan payment? And are you ready to make a long-term financial commitment?

____ Start looking for a home in your price range.

C. On a separate sheet of paper, write a paragraph about how to buy a house using the information above. Remember to start with a topic sentence and use transitions to connect your ideas.

Name: _____
Date: _____

Analyze an Ad

The <u>Best Computer</u> Around!
A COMPLETE Package!

The Fastest!
The Cheapest!* ($1200)
The Biggest Hard Drive! (1.8 GigaHertz)

Take it for a Test Drive!
(If you're not completely satisfied within 30 days, we'll give you your money back!)**

*Monitor and printer are sold separately, shipping and handling not included.
**You must pay for shipping and handling to return the computer.

Complete the following statements about the advertising techniques this company is using.

1. The ad is attractive because _____

2. The ad tries to pull you in by _____

3. It persuades you to think that _____

4. I wouldn't trust this ad because _____

5. I would try to find out the truth by _____

6. Some information that is not included is _____

Name: _____

Date: _____

Complaints

A. Listen to each conversation and fill in the table with the information you hear.

	Conversation #1	Conversation #2	Conversation #3
Where is the customer?			
What is the complaint?			
What does the customer want?			
Does the customer get what he or she wants?			
Does the employee give good customer service?			

B. Choose one of the situations above and write the conversation between the customer and the employee. Use your own words.

Customer: _____

Employee: _____

Customer: _____

Employee: _____

Customer: _____

Employee: _____

Customer: _____

Employee: _____

Customer: _____

Employee: _____

C. Practice your conversation with a partner.

Unit 3: Active Tasks

1. Complete each Active Task.
2. Write the date you completed the task.
3. Write down the people you spoke to, the information you gathered, or the Internet addresses where you found information.
4. Write down your personal thoughts about the experience.

Lesson	Active Task	Action Date	People I Spoke To	Information I Gathered	Personal Thoughts
1	Read some housing ads in the newspaper or on the Internet. Make a list of any words or abbreviations you don't understand and try to work out the meanings.				
5	Use the Internet or the newspaper to find out about real estate agents in your area. What kind of services do they offer? What kind of fees do they charge?				

Name: _____
Date: _____

Homes for Sale

A. The two homes for sale below are in the same price range. Read the ads.

> Perfect for a young family! Come see this spacious 2-bedroom 2 ½-bath town home in a gated community. This two-story town home has a loft and vaulted ceilings in every room. Other amenities include 2-car garage, air-conditioning, large patio/deck, working fireplace, Jacuzzi, and a pool. Other units in this neighborhood are selling like hotcakes! Come see it while it lasts! Low monthly association dues. Offered at $259,000.

> This fixer-upper is waiting for you! Four bedrooms and 3 ½ baths with a large living area and huge kitchen. Backyard has a pool, large grassy area and even a tree house! Three-car garage and a driveway that will hold 6 more cars. What more could you want? Near schools and bus stops. A perfect project for the artist in you! Come see it today! $250,000

B. What do these words and expressions mean?

association dues: _____

fixer-upper: _____

loft : _____

selling like hotcakes: _____

spacious: _____

vaulted ceilings: _____

Name: _____

Date: _____

C. Answer the questions.

1. One house is bigger than the other, but they are priced about the same. Why?

_____

_____

_____

2. In your opinion, which home is a better deal? Why?

_____

_____

_____

3. Which home would you rather buy? Why?

_____

_____

_____

Name: _____

Date: _____

Comparative and Superlative Adjectives

A. Write the comparative and superlative form of each adjective below.

Adjective	Comparative	Superlative
bright	*brighter*	*the brightest*
cheap		
clean		
close		
dangerous		
dark		
dirty		
expensive		
happy		
light		
mountainous		
new		
old		
peaceful		
poor		
quiet		
safe		
small		
strong		
suburban		
urban		
wealthy		

B. Using adjectives from the previous page, write sentences comparing the town home and the house.

TOWN HOME
Perfect for a young family! Come see this spacious 2 bedroom 2 ½ bath town home in a safe city neighborhood. This two-story town home has a loft and vaulted ceilings in every room. Other amenities include 2-car garage, air-conditioning, large patio/deck, wood-burning fireplace, gated community with a Jacuzzi and pool. Other units in this neighborhood are selling like hotcakes! Come see it while it lasts! Low monthly association dues. Offered at $259,000.

HOUSE
This fixer-upper is waiting for you! Four bedrooms and 3 ½ baths with a large living area and huge kitchen. Backyard has a pool, large grassy area and even a tree house! Three-car garage and a driveway that will hold 6 more cars. What more could you want? Near schools and bus stops. A perfect project for the artist in you! Come see it today! $250,000

1. _____

2. _____

3. _____

4. _____

5. _____

Name: _____
Date: _____

Compare the Homes

A. Read the sentences and put the homes in order from most expensive to cheapest.

The Castle is more expensive than the Mansion and the Rural Ranch.
The Studio is less expensive than the Apartment.
The Mobile Home is more expensive than the Apartment.
The Townhome is cheaper than the Suburban Home and the Rural Ranch.
The City Condo is more expensive than the Houseboat.
The Houseboat is more expensive the Mobile Home.
The Rural Ranch is cheaper than the Mansion but more expensive than the Suburban Home.
The Townhome is more expensive than the City Condo.

1. _____   6. _____
2. _____   7. _____
3. _____   8. _____
4. _____   9. _____
5. _____   10. _____

B. Read the sentences and put the homes in order from largest to smallest.

The Beach Condo is larger than the Hotel Suite.
The Farm is larger than the Palace and the Harbor Home.
The Shoebox is smaller than the Cottage.
The Town House is larger the Flat.
The Flat is larger than the Cottage.
The Beach Condo is smaller the Mountain Cabin and the Harbor Home.
The Hotel Suite is larger than the Town House.
The Harbor Home is smaller than the Palace but larger than the Mountain Cabin.

1. _____   6. _____
2. _____   7. _____
3. _____   8. _____
4. _____   9. _____
5. _____   10. _____

Comparative and Superlative Questions

A. Complete each question with the correct form of the verb: *be* or *have*.

1. Which house _____ bigger?

2. Which apartment _____ more space?

3. Which ones _____ yards?

4. Which place _____ closer to your job?

5. Which house _____ the most bathrooms?

6. Which studios _____ kitchens?

7. Which mobile home _____ closer to the beach?

8. Which place _____ more rooms?

9. Which condo _____ the cheapest?

10. What homes _____ closer to the good schools?

B. Write comparative and superlative questions using the words given below.

1. apartment   space

_____

2. town house   expensive

_____

3. mobile home   big yard

_____

4. building   cheap rent

_____

5. studio   small

_____

Yes/No Questions

A. Rewrite each of the following statements as a yes/no question.

1.   Nury wants to move into a four-bedroom townhouse.
      Does Nury want to move into a four-bedroom townhouse? _____

2.   Sam hopes to buy a new home for his mother.
      _____

3.   The children like to play in their new yard.
      _____

4.   The roof on the building needs to be repaired.
      _____

5.   Alex and Logan have a two-bedroom apartment.
      _____

6.   The advertisements don't have phone numbers.
      _____

7.   You live near the freeway and the college.
      _____

8.   The family likes their safe neighborhood.
      _____

9.   Dana wants a place with a yard for her puppies.
      _____

10.   The Internet has the best classified ads.
      _____

Bonus Questions:
11.   Bob built his house on a new lot.
      _____

12.   The company tore down the house to build a new one.
      _____

B. With a partner, practice asking and answering the questions you wrote.
Example:
      Student A: *Does Nury want to move into a four-bedroom townhouse?*
      Student B: *Yes, she does.*

C. Answer the following questions with short answers.

Example: Do you live in California?
             Yes, I do. _____

1.   Do you live in an apartment?_____

2.   Do you live in a house?_____

3.   Do you live alone?_____

4.   Do you live with your family?_____

5.   Do you live with your friends?_____

6.   Does your family live in the United States?_____

7.   Do you own a home?_____

8.   Do you want to own a home?_____

9.   Does your home have at least two bedrooms?_____

10.   Does the President of the United States live in the White House?

      _____

11.   Does the leader of your country live in the White House? _____

12.   Does your teacher live in the city your school is in?_____

13.   Do some of your classmates live near you?_____

14.   Do you want to move to a new home?_____

Information Questions

A. Write a question that asks about the underlined part of the sentence.

Example: Their family needs <u>three bedrooms</u>.
How many bedrooms does their family need?

1. I want to buy <u>a house</u>.
_____

2. The newlyweds want to live <u>in Montana</u>.
_____

3. Their price range is <u>$125,000 - $150,000</u>.
_____

4. The house has <u>five bedrooms</u>.
_____

5. The couple is prepared to put down <u>ten percent</u>.
_____

6. They got approved for their loan <u>last week</u>.
_____

7. The condominium costs <u>$135,000</u>.
_____

8. The house he wants to buy is <u>in a bad neighborhood</u>.
_____

9. The sisters are thinking of moving <u>closer to their mother</u>.
_____

10. I intend to buy <u>a new home</u> next year.
_____

A Business Letter

Below are eight parts of a business letter. Decide which part of the letter goes where and rewrite the letter on the next page.

Dear Home Central,

I have decided to purchase a new home and I need some help. I would like a two-bedroom place in the city close to my job. I would prefer a home with an enclosed yard or a balcony for my dog. Air conditioning, washer/dryer hookups, and a garage are a must.

19782 Hermosa Lane
Hermosa Beach, CA 90254

February 13, 2002

Home Central
9280 Pier Street
Hermosa Beach, CA 90254

Sincerely,

Wendy Willis

I'm willing to spend between $150, 000 and $200, 000 and I am prepared to put down 20%. If someone at your office is willing to help me search for my new home, please contact me at the address above or you may call me at work (310) 555-4553. Thank you for your time.

Wendy Willis

Name: _____

Date: _____

Name: _____

Date: _____

Housing Bar Graph

A. What are the different types of places you can live in? Make a list.

_____   _____

_____   _____

_____   _____

_____   _____

B. Now take a poll of your class and find out how many students live in each place. Write the numbers in the chart below.

Place	Number of Students	Percentage of Students

C. Now calculate the percentage of students. Look at the example below. Write the percentages in the chart above.

Example:

15 students live in apartments

35 students in class

$$\frac{15}{35} = 42.8\%$$

D. Write the types of housing along the bottom of the graph. Draw bars that show the percentages you calculated in exercise B.

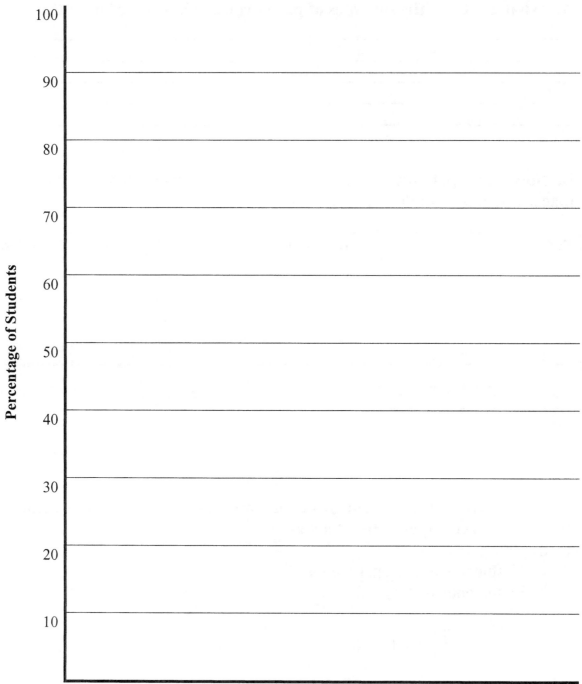

Housing Types

Reading Comprehension & Vocabulary

A. Turn to pages 55-56 in your student book. Skim the article quickly.

B. Answer the following questions about the article.

1. What is the first thing homebuyers do?
   A. Have the home inspected.
   B. Make an offer on a home.
   C. Find out how much they can afford.
   D. Process the loan.

2. According to the article, what is the best way to do your own cost comparison?
   A. Ask your friends.
   B. Look on the Internet.
   C. Look in the newspaper.
   D. Look up recent sales of comparable properties in public records.

3. When do you make an offer?
   A. once you've found a property that you like and can afford
   B. the first time you see the house
   C. after you have the house inspected
   D. before you find your real estate agent

4. When does the inspection take place?
   A. before you make an offer
   B. after the purchase contract has been signed
   C. after you move into the house
   D. a year after you have lived in the house

C. Go through the article again and underline any words you still don't understand. Make a list below and ask a classmate for the meanings or look them up in a dictionary.

Words I Need to Study	Part of Speech	Definition
1.		
2.		
3.		
4.		
5.		
6.		
7.		
8.		
9.		
10.		

Name: _____
Date: _____

Unit 4: Active Tasks

1. Complete each Active Task.
2. Write the date you completed the task.
3. Write down the people you spoke to, the information you gathered, or the Internet addresses where you found information
4. Write down your personal thoughts about the experience.

Lesson	Active Task	Action Date	People I Spoke To	Information I Gathered	Personal Thoughts
1	Use the phone book or the Internet to find other locations to do the activities on page 62 in your book. Report back to the class.				
2	Make an appointment with a school counselor and ask him or her the questions you wrote. Then report back to the class.				
3	Go to a community center and look at the bulletin board. Make a list of activities posted and report back to your class.				

Unit 4
Active Task Checklist

Lesson	Active Task	Action Date	People I Spoke To	Information I Gathered	Personal Thoughts
4	Visit your local library and find out about their services. Ask the librarian some of the questions you wrote above and report back to the class.				
5	Call up your local supermarket or bookstore and ask for directions from your house. Write them down.				
6	Find the phone number and/or address of two places you might volunteer in your phone directory or on the Internet. Visit the location or call and talk to someone. Ask them your three questions. Volunteer to help!				
7	Go to the Visitor's Bureau in your city or look on the Internet to find a Visitor's Guide for your city. What information does it have?				

Name: _____

Date: _____

Class Telephone Directory

A. For this activity, you will create a class telephone directory, based on places in your community. With a group of four or five students, complete the table below with names of places you gathered from your community.

Education	Employment	Health

Local Government	Recreation	Transportation

B. For each of the places you listed above, find the complete name, address, and phone number. You may have to do some research to find this information (phone book, the Internet, etc.)

C. Create your class telephone directory.

1. Combine the information from every group.

2. Put the places in alphabetical order.

3. Write the information in your telephone directory on the next page.

Optional: Create your telephone directory on the computer.

Name: _____

Date: _____

Telephone Directory

Place	Address	Phone Number

Embedded Questions

> **Would/Will/Could/Can you tell me…..?**
> **Would/Will/Could/Can you explain…..?**
> **Would/Will/Could/Can you show me…..?**
> **Do you know…..?**

A. Write embedded questions for each of the examples below.

<u>TIME</u>

1. class starts

_____

2. the bookstore closes

_____

3. your plane leaves

_____

4. the bus arrives

_____

<u>LOCATION</u>

5. the library

_____

6. the park

_____

7. a gym

_____

8. a good pizza place

_____

Name: _____

Date: _____

INFORMATION

9. the name of our teacher

_____

10. the cost of our book

_____

11. a good movie that's out right now

_____

12. how to register for college classes

_____

B. Practice asking and answering the questions you wrote with a partner. Your partner will have to come up with answers to each of your questions.

C. Combine the two questions to make an embedded question.

1. Do you know? How often does the bus come?

_____

2. Can you explain to me? How does the scanner work?

_____

3. Will you show me? Where is the bank?

_____

4. Do you know? Does the shoe store sell children's shoes?

_____

5. Would you tell me? Do you know of a place I can volunteer?

_____

6. Could you tell me? Is the school open this Saturday?

_____

Making Suggestions

Making Suggestions	Responding to Suggestions
Why don't you......?	That a great idea!
You could......	Great! Thanks for the suggestion.
How about......?	I've already tried that. Can you think of something else?

A. Ask your partner for suggestions about places to go in your community.

Example: You: Where can I buy the book for this class?
            Partner: Why don't you go to the school bookstore?
            You: That's a great idea!

1. I need to get in shape.

2. Do you know of a good general practice doctor?

3. I need to get a birthday gift for my 12-year-old son.

4. I've always wanted to learn how to play an instrument.

5. My mechanic is moving and I don't know where I'm going to get my car repaired.

6. I'm looking for a place to get fresh fruits and vegetables.

7. Do you know of a good restaurant near our school?

B. What did your partner say? Write his or her suggestions below.

Example: *My partner suggested I go to the school bookstore.*

1. _____

2. _____

3. _____

4. _____

5. _____

6. _____

7. _____

Name: _____

Date: _____

Internet Access at the Library

FREE INTERNET ACCESS
For Loronado Public Library cardholders in the computer lab located in the Media Room

NEW HOURS
Monday 1:00 p.m. – 8:45 p.m.
Tuesday 10:15 a.m. – 8:45 p.m.
Wednesday 10:15 a.m. – 6:45 p.m.
Thursday 10:15 a.m. – 6:45 p.m.
Friday 11:00 a.m. – 4:45 p.m.
Saturday 11:00 a.m. – 4:45 p.m.
Sunday 1:00 p.m. – 4:45 p.m.
Hours may change without notice.

Media Room Computer Lab Policies

USERS
All users need their Loronado Public Library card along with a photo ID to access the computers. You must be 12 years or older, or be accompanied by an adult, to use the Computer Lab. There are computers for those under 12 years in the Children's Reading Room.

TIME LIMITS and RESERVATIONS
Computers are available on a first come, first served basis. You are limited to 60 minutes per day. We do not take reservations.

CONDUCT
No food or drink is allowed in the Computer Lab. When using the Internet at the Library, YOU MAY NOT:
• Load personal software on the computers.
• Use the Internet for any illegal activity.
• Invade someone's personal privacy.

Misuse of the computer or Internet access will result in loss of your computer privileges.

SAVING/DOWNLOADING
If you wish to save files, bring your own disk, formatted for an IBM PC compatible. You can purchase a disk for $1 at the library.

WARNING: FILES DOWNLOADED FROM THE INTERNET MAY CONTAIN A VIRUS. YOU NEED TO HAVE VIRUS CHECKING SOFTWARE LOADED ON YOUR COMPUTER TO AVOID A VIRUS.

PRINTING
Printing is 15 cents per page with a copy card. Please pick up printing at the Media Room front desk.

A. Read the information on Internet access at Loronado Public Library and answer the following questions.

1. How much time can you spend on a computer?
2. Can you save things from the Internet? If yes, how?
3. How much does it cost to print a page? Where do you pick up the pages?
4. When can you use the computers on Friday?
5. Who is allowed to use the computers in the computer lab?
6. Can you put your own software on the library computers?

Name: _____

Date: _____

Calling for Directions

A. When you write down directions, you can use *shorthand* to take notes. Look at the shorthand symbols below.

south	**S**	left	**L**
north	**N**	right	**R**
east	**E**	miles	**mi.**
west	**W**		

B. Look at the directions below written in shorthand. How would you read these directions to someone? Discuss with a partner.

42 E
94 W
exit Laura Lane R
Grover St L
2 mi
Kitchner R
on L side

C. Listen to each person call and ask for directions. Write down where they are coming from, where they are going to and the directions. Use shorthand to write the directions.

Conversation 1:

Going To	Directions
Coming From	

Name: _____

Date: _____

Conversation 2:

Going To	Directions
Coming From	

Conversation 3:

Going To	Directions
Coming From	

D. Share your directions with a partner. Did you write down the same thing?

E. Choose one set of directions that you wrote above and draw a map of those directions in the box below.

Name: _____

Date: _____

Volunteer at the Animal Shelter

A. Read the article below that appeared in last week's newspaper.

Hundreds of pets are found each week roaming the streets, looking for food and love. Some of them ran away from home. Some of them got lost. Many of them were left. Still others were born out on the streets and have never had a home. Each day we pick up so many dogs and cats and bring them back to our shelter to help them get healthy again. And our ultimate goal here at Grady's Animal Shelter is to find each and every one of them a loving home. But in the meantime, we need your help.

Have you ever wanted to give back to your community? Do you have a few hours a week to spare that you'd like to do something worthwhile with, something that will make you feel good about yourself? We need you! Here at Grady's we strive to give every pet as much love as we can by spending time with each and every one of them for at least a few hours a day. How can you help?

Maybe you like to exercise and would like to take our dogs for a run or walk. Perhaps you would like to play with the dogs by taking them to the park and throwing a ball or Frisbee. Maybe you'd like to help us feed the pets and clean their cages. Maybe you would like to sit and pet the cats or snuggle with the puppies. Whatever you do best, we'll find something for you to do here at Grady's. We guarantee you'll feel good every time you're here. And maybe you'll even find a new friend to adopt!

Make it a family project! Children are great caregivers to animals and with your supervision, your kids can get a lot out of volunteering. Teach them what it means to give back, and spend some family time while you're at it!

Are you ready to help? Do you still have some more questions? Call us today at (619) 555-9028 or stop by and see us at 4837 Feline Way. We're all waiting for you!

B. Answer the questions below based on what you read.

1. Who can volunteer at Grady's Animal Shelter?
    A. adults
    B. dogs and cats
    C. children
    D. both A and C

2. What is NOT something you can do with the pets?
    A. play in the park
    B. feed them
    C. give them a bath
    D. take them for a walk

3. What is Grady's main goal?
    A. to get the animals off the streets
    B. to find each pet a home
    C. to give each animal love
    D. to feed the animals

4. How many hours do you have to volunteer?
    A. a few a week
    B. a few a day
    C. a few a month
    D. the article doesn't say

Name: _____

Date: _____

C. Look back in the reading and underline each of the expressions below.

a few hours a week to spare

do something worthwhile

family project

get a lot out of

give back

in the meantime

roaming the streets

spend some family time

whatever you do best

D. What do you think the expressions mean? Discuss them with a partner and make notes next to each one about the meaning. Go over them with your class if you still don't understand.

E. Choose two of the expressions above and write two sentences about volunteering.

1. _____

   _____

2. _____

   _____

Visitor's Guide

A. Read the Visitor's Guide below. What information is missing?

Loronado Visitor's Guide

Loronado has been around since _____.

Now it has _____ people.

Little Blue Bus

Price: _____
Stops at: _____ locations

Loronado Players

Performance: _____
Days: _____
Time: _____
Price for adults: _____
Price for seniors: _____
Price for children: _____

Maritime Art Museum

Location: _____
Hours: _____

Relax!

Where: _____

Shops

Location: _____
Days: Monday-Friday
Hours: _____
Days: _____
Hours: _____

Sunset Park

What can you do there?

_____

Price: _____

B. Listen to the Visitor's Guide on Loronado. Fill in the missing information.

Name: _____

Date: _____

Read for Information

A. Read the Visitor's Guide below.

Welcome to historic Loronado! Loronado has been around since 1910 when the first settlers came to live near the water. It started out with just one main street and now it has grown into a large metropolis with over 200, 000 people! We're so glad you chose Loronado as your vacation destination and we'd like to tell you about some of the fun things you can do.

First of all, to get an overview of the whole city, hop on the Little Blue Bus. This is a small trolley car that will take you all around the city and show you the sights. For only $5, you can stay on the Little Blue Bus all day. It stops at 10 different locations where you can get off and then get back on when you're ready to go to the next spot. This gives you a great overview of Loronado and will give you an idea of where you'd like to spend more time.

For all you art lovers out there, Loronado has a world famous art museum where many famous maritime paintings are housed. It's located on Grant Avenue in an old lighthouse. The museum is open daily from 10 to 4 and I promise you won't be disappointed!

I'm sure we have some shoppers out there. You should head over to Main Street where you'll find tons of clothing boutiques, book shops, music stores, antiques, and gift shops. Most of the stores are open Monday through Friday from 10AM to 9PM and Saturday and Sunday from 12-5PM.

Come one, come all! The Loronado Players are in town doing a performance of Oklahoma! The Players perform in an old movie theater that has been renovated and it's a show that you won't want to miss. They perform every night except Monday at 8PM. Rush on over to get your tickets. Adults $45, seniors and children $25.

For those of you who just like to relax, take a stroll down by the water. Loronado is famous for its beautiful beaches and ocean breezes.

Kids, don't think we have forgotten about you. Head down to Sunset Park where there are rides and games every Saturday and Sunday. Spend the whole day there for just $10 and meet some new friends.

These are just a few things you can do while you're in town. For more information please visit our Visitor's Bureau. And don't forget to have a great time!

Name: _____

Date: _____

B. Imagine that you really want to do each of the things listed on the previous page. For each place or thing to do listed below, what information is missing? (For example: times, locations, price, etc.) Write a question you could ask to get the information you need.

Little Blue Bus

Missing information: _____

Question I could ask: _____

_____

Art Museum

Missing information: _____

Question I could ask: _____

_____

Loronado Players

Missing information: _____

Question I could ask: _____

_____

Relax by the Water

Missing information: _____

Question I could ask: _____

_____

Sunset Park

Missing information: _____

Question I could ask: _____

_____

Name:

Date:

Unit 5
Active Task Checklist

Unit 5: Active Tasks

1. Complete each Active Task.
2. Write the date you completed the task.
3. Write down the people you spoke to, the information you gathered, or the Internet addresses where you found information.
4. Write down your personal thoughts about the experience.

Lesson	Active Task	Action Date	People I Spoke To	Information I Gathered	Personal Thoughts
1	Take a poll among your family and friends of their good health habits. Make a bar graph.				
3	Think of a conversation you had recently with a friend, family member, co-worker, or your teacher. Tell your partner what the person said to you.				
4	Find a health insurance application form from a health insurance company or from the Internet. Fill out the application.				

Heinle © 2002
Stand Out 4 Activity Bank

Unit 5
Active Task Checklist

Name: _____
Date: _____

Lesson	Active Task	Action Date	People I Spoke To	Information I Gathered	Personal Thoughts
5	Read the food labels of your favorite products or look them up on the Internet. Share the information with your class.				
6	At home or on the Internet, look at the labels of drugs that you or your family members take. Answer the questions on page 93 in your book for each drug.				
7	Find an interesting article in the newspaper or on the Internet. Write a summary using the guidelines on page 96 in your book.				

Name: _____

Date: _____

Healthy vs. Unhealthy

A.   Listen to each person talk about his or her health habits. Check healthy or unhealthy.

Example: I'm addicted to cola. I probably drink at least four cans a day.
  ❑ healthy   ❑ unhealthy

1. ❑ healthy ❑ unhealthy   6. ❑ healthy ❑ unhealthy

2. ❑ healthy ❑ unhealthy   7. ❑ healthy ❑ unhealthy

3. ❑ healthy ❑ unhealthy   8. ❑ healthy ❑ unhealthy

4. ❑ healthy ❑ unhealthy   9. ❑ healthy ❑ unhealthy

5. ❑ healthy ❑ unhealthy   10.❑ healthy ❑ unhealthy

B. Listen to the people again. What are their habits? Write them below.

Example: _drinking cola_

1. _____

2. _____

3. _____

4. _____

5. _____

6. _____

7. _____

8. _____

9. _____

10. _____

Name: _____
Date: _____

My Health Habits

A. Answer the questions about your health habits.

	Days

1. How many days a week do you eat *healthy food*?
2. How many days a week do you *NOT smoke*?
3. How many days a week do you *NOT drink alcohol*?
4. How many days a week do you get at least *8 hours of sleep*?
5. How many days a week do you *exercise*?
6. How many days a week do you *drink water*?

B. Write the habits from the questions above at the bottom of the graph. Write the number of days on the left side of the graph. Shade in the bar graph based on your answers above.

2					
1					
	healthy food				

C. Would you consider your habits healthy or unhealthy? Why?

Present Perfect and Present Perfect Continuous

A. Make sentences using the *present perfect* or *present perfect continuous* and *for* or *since*.

1. my neck hurts / two days

   _____

2. my children have a cold / Friday

   _____

3. Peter is sick / two weeks

   _____

4. they are not speaking / 6pm

   _____

5. she is not feeling well / yesterday

   _____

6. Brian's leg hurts/ last night

   _____

7. how long / Ella feels dizzy

   _____

8. I have a limp / I was a child

   _____

9. the girls aren't sleeping well / two weeks

   _____

10. her son has a learning disability/ he was 3 years old.

    _____

11. Ismael studies medicine / four years

    _____

12. his parents are at the hospital / this morning

    _____

B.   Answer each question with a complete sentence.

1. How long have you lived in this city?

_____

2. How long have you been studying English?

_____

3. How long have you been in this class?

_____

4. How long have you been going to this school?

_____

C. Ask a partner the same questions that you just answered above. Write his or her answers in complete sentences below.

1. _____

2. _____

3. _____

4. _____

Indirect Speech

A. Change each of the following quotations to an indirect speech statement.

Example: "You should wash your hands before you eat dinner," my mother said.
My mother said that I should wash my hands before I eat dinner.

1. "You should do these back exercises three times a week," my physical therapist told me.

_____

_____

2. "Walking is the best way to bring down your blood pressure," my friend's doctor said.

_____

_____

3. His chiropractor warned him, "Bad posture while you are sitting at your desk will make your back problems worse."

_____

_____

4. "All of your tests came back negative and you seem to be in perfect health!" exclaimed my doctor.

_____

_____

B. Ask your partner each of the questions below and write his or her answer as an indirect speech statement.

1. What is your healthiest habit?

_____

_____

2. What is your unhealthiest habit?

_____

_____

3. What food should you eat more of?

_____

_____

4. What is your favorite kind of exercise?

_____

_____

Healthy Life HMO

A. Discuss the following questions with a small group.

1. What is the difference between an HMO (health maintenance organization) and a PPO (preferred provider organization)?
2. Do you have health insurance? If so, do you have an HMO or a PPO?
3. Who pays for your health insurance or medical costs?
4. Are you satisfied with your medical coverage?

B. Read about Healthy Life HMO.

Healthy Life HMO: An Overview

Welcome to Healthy Life HMO! You or your employer has chosen us to take care of your medical needs. HMO stands for health maintenance organization and that's exactly what we intend to do – maintain your health. Our well-trained medical staff is prepared to meet all of your needs.

At Healthy Life, you will choose one medical group that you will see for all your medical requests. This medical group can be chosen from a list of service providers in your area. You may see any doctor within that group. If the doctor in your group doesn't specialize in the area of medical attention that you need, he or she will recommend and refer you to another doctor. Once this paperwork has been processed, you are free to make an appointment with that doctor. This doctor will report all of his or her findings as well as any services provided back to your original doctor so we can keep your file up to date.

Every time you visit the doctor, you will be required to pay a $10 co-pay. This is all you have to pay if the service you are requesting is part of your insurance policy*. Some services are covered 100% while others are only partially covered. If the service is only partially covered, Healthy Life will send you a bill in the mail for the portion you have to pay. You will then have 30 days to remit your payment for services rendered.

Once you have finished reading through the policy that is attached, please choose a medical group. Then call us so we can process the paperwork and put you on file with that group. This can take up to a month so don't delay in making your choice. If you decide later that you wish to change medical groups, you will have a window of opportunity to make this change every year.

Thank you for choosing Healthy Life. We look forward to serving you and keeping you healthy!

*Please see your individual policy for what is and what is not covered.

C. Find the following vocabulary expressions in the reading. What do you think each one means? Make inferences by looking at the words around each expression.

co-pay	
partially covered	
process the paperwork	
remit your payment	
services provided	
services rendered	
specialize	
window of opportunity	

D. Answer each of the following questions based on the reading.

1. What does HMO stand for?

_____

2. Can you go to any doctor you want to? How do you have to choose a doctor?

_____

3. What do you have to do if you want to see a special doctor who is not in your medical group?

_____

4. How much do you have to pay when you go to the doctor?

_____

5. If the insurance company sends you a bill, when is the payment due?

_____

6. What if you want to change medical groups?

_____

Name: _____
Date: _____

Nutrition Label Practice 1

CANNED BAKED BEANS

Nutrition Facts
Serving Size 1 cup
Can = 2 cups
Amount Per Serving
Calories 236.2   Calories from Fat 9.6

	% Daily Value
Total Fat 1.1g	2%
Saturated Fat 0.3g	1%
Polyunsaturated Fat 0.5g	
Monounsaturated Fat 0.1g	
Cholesterol 0mg	0%
Sodium 1,008.4mg	42%
Protein 12.2g	
Total Carbohydrate 52.1g	17%
Dietary Fiber 12.7g	51%
Sugars N/A	

Read the nutrition label and answer the questions.

1. How much fat is in one serving of beans? _____

2. How many of the calories are from fat? _____

3. Are there any carbohydrates in the beans? _____ If so, how many grams? _____

4. How much sodium is in one serving of beans? _____

5. How much sugar is in one serving? _____

6. How many calories are in 2 servings of beans? _____

7. How many servings are in this can? _____

8. Are the beans high in protein? _____

9. Would it be good to eat these beans if you are watching your cholesterol? _____

10. Are these beans a good source of dietary fiber? _____

Name: _____
Date: _____

Nutrition Label Practice 2

Oat Cereal

Nutrition Facts
Serving Size 1/2 cup
Box = 4 cups
Amount Per Serving
Calories 218.3   Calories from Fat 62.6

	% Daily Value
Total Fat 7.3g	11%
Saturated Fat 3.2g	16%
Polyunsaturated Fat 0.8g	
Monounsaturated Fat 3.2g	
Cholesterol 0.5mg	0%
Sodium 11.2mg	0%
Protein 4.8g	
Total Carbohydrate 35.8g	12%
Dietary Fiber 3.7g	15%
Sugars N/A	

Read the nutrition label and answer the questions.

1. How much fat is in one serving of cereal? _____

2. How many of the calories are from fat? _____

3. Are there any carbohydrates in the cereal? _____ If so, how many grams? _____

4. How much sodium is in one serving of cereal? _____

5. How much sugar is in one serving? _____

6. How many calories are in two servings of cereal? _____

7. How many servings are in this box? _____

8. Is the cereal high in protein? _____

9. Would it be good to eat this cereal if you are watching your sodium intake? _____

10. Is this cereal a good source of dietary fiber? _____

Nutrition Label Practice 3

Low Fat Fruit Yogurt

Nutrition Facts
Serving Size 8 oz

Amount per serving
Calories 249.6 cal   **Calories from Fat**   48

	% Daily Value*
Total Fat 2.6 g	2%
Saturated Fat 1.7 g	3%
Polyunsaturated Fat 0.1 g	
Monounsaturated Fat 0.7 g	
Cholesterol 10.3 mg	1%
Sodium 143.1 mg	2%
Total Carbohydrates 46.7 g	6%
Dietary Fiber 0 g	0%
Sugars 46.7g	
Protein 10.7 g	

*Recommended Daily Allowances

	Calories	2000	2500
Total Fat	Less than	65g	80g
Sat Fat	Less than	20g	25g
Cholesterol	Less than	300mg	300mg
Sodium	Less than	2400mg	2400mg
Total Carbohydrate		300g	375g
Dietary Fiber		25g	30g

Read the nutrition label and answer the questions.

1. How much fat is in one serving of yogurt? _____ What percent of your daily allowance is this? _____
2. How many of the calories are from fat? _____
3. Are there any carbohydrates in the yogurt? _____ If so, how many? _____
4. How much sodium is in one serving of yogurt? _____
5. How much sugar is in one serving? _____
6. How many calories are in three servings of yogurt? _____
7. What is your daily recommended allowance of saturated fat? _____ What is the percentage of your daily allowance in 8oz of yogurt? _____
8. Is the yogurt high in protein? _____
9. Would it be good to eat this yogurt if you are watching your fat intake? _____
10. Is this yogurt a good source of dietary fiber? _____

Name: _____

Date: _____

Nutrition Label Quiz

Crackers

Nutrition Facts
Serving Size 18 crackers (29 g)
Servings Per Container About 9
Amount Per Serving
Calories 120   Calories from Fat 30
% Daily Value
Total Fat 4g   **6%**
Saturated Fat 0.5g   **3%**
Polyunsaturated Fat 0g
Monounsaturated Fat 1g
Cholesterol 0mg **0%**
Sodium 120mg **5%**
Protein 1g
Total Carbohydrate 20g **7%**
Dietary Fiber 1g **6%**
Sugars 13g
Vitamin A 0%   Vitamin C 0%
Calcium 0%   Iron C 0%

Read the nutrition label and circle the correct answer.

1. How much fat is in one serving of crackers?
   a. 1g   b. .5g   c. 4g   d. 6g

2. How many of the calories are from fat?
   a. 30   b. 120   c. 9   d. 4

3. Are there any vitamins in the crackers?
   a. yes   b. no   c. it doesn't say

4. How much sugar is in one serving of crackers?
   a. 13g   b. 1g   c. 6%   d. 20 g

5. How much sugar is in the whole box of crackers?
   a. 13g   b. 20 g   c. 1g   d. 117g

6. How many carbohydrates are in 2 servings of crackers?
   a. 20g   b. 40g   c. 60g   d. 30g

7. How many servings are in this box?
   a. 29g   b.   120   c. 9   d. 18 crackers

8. Are the crackers high in protein?
   a. yes   b. no

9. Would it be good to eat these crackers if you are watching your cholesterol?
   a. yes   b. no

10. Are these crackers a good source of vitamin C?
   a. yes   b. no

Medicine Label Practice 1

Cold/Flu Relief Syrup	
USES Temporarily relieves common cold/ flu symptoms: <ul><li>coughing</li><li>fever</li><li>headaches</li><li>muscular aches</li><li>nasal congestion</li><li>pains</li><li>runny nose</li><li>sneezing</li><li>sore throat</li></ul>	**DIRECTIONS** 12 years and older: Take 2 tablespoons. Repeat every 6 hours if necessary. Do not take more that 4 doses a day. **WARNING** **Do not exceed recommended dosage.** If nervousness, dizziness, or sleeplessness occur, stop taking and consult your physician. May cause drowsiness. May cause excitability in children. **ALCOHOL WARNING** If you consume more than three alcoholic drinks per day, ask your doctor whether you can take this medicine. **Keep this drug out of the reach of children.** In case of accidental overdose, get professional advice or contact poison control right away.

Read the medicine label and answer the following questions.

1. What age person can take this medicine?
_____

2. How many doses of this medicine can you take in one day?
_____

3. What should you do if you take too much of this medicine?
_____

4. What are three symptoms this medicine will relieve?
_____

5. What should you do if you feel dizzy after you take this medicine?
_____

6. What is the recommended dosage of this medicine?
_____

7. How often can you take it?
_____

8. What does the alcohol warning on this medicine mean?
_____
_____

Name: _____
Date: _____

Medicine Label Practice 2

Mouth Sore Medication
Directions: Adults and children over 2 years: Dry the sore area. Apply medication to affected area. Use up to 4 times a day or as recommended by your doctor. Do not use more than once every 2 hours. Children under 12 years of age should be supervised in the use of this medication. **Caution:** Avoid contact with eyes. Do not use the product for more than 7 days unless directed by a physician. If irritation, pain or redness continues or worsens or if a rash or fever develops, discontinue use and contact your physician immediately.

Read the medicine label and answer the following questions.

1. What age person can take this medicine?

   _____

2. How many doses of this medicine can you take in one day?

   _____

3. What should you do if this medicine causes a rash?

   _____

4. What symptoms will this medicine relieve?

   _____

5. How many days can you take this medication?

   _____

6. What are the directions for using the medication?

   _____

   _____

7. How often can you take it?

   _____

Medicine Label Practice 3

Nasal Spray
▪ moisturizes dry, irritated noses ▪ clears stuffy noses fast ▪ last for up to 12 hours Directions: Adults and children 6 to under 12 years of age (with supervisions): 2-3 sprays in each nostril not more than every 10 to 12 hours. Do not exceed 2 doses in a 24-hour period. Children under 6 years old: consult a doctor. To spray, squeeze bottle quickly and firmly. Do not tilt head backward while spraying. Wipe nozzle after use. Warnings: No not exceed recommended dosage. Do not use for more than 3 days. Use of this container by more than one person may spread infection.

Read the medicine label and answer the following questions.

1. How long will one dose of this medicine lasts?

   _____

2. Why would you take this medicine?

   _____

3. Can children take this medication?

   _____

4. What symptoms will this medicine relieve?

   _____

5. How many days can you take this medication?

   _____

6. What are the directions for using the medication?

   _____

   _____

7. What will happen if more than one person uses this spray?

   _____

Summary Writing Checklist

A. Find an article in the newspaper, on the Internet, or in your book that is interesting to you and write a summary using the guidelines on page 96 of your student book.

B. Use the checklist below to edit your summary. If you marked *No*, then go back to your summary and fix it. Put a check in the *Fixed* box.

	Yes	No	Fixed
1. Did you mention the author and the title of the article?			
2. Did you identify the main idea at the beginning of your summary?			
3. Did you include all the important points?			
4. Did you leave out the unnecessary details?			
5. Did you write the ideas in the order in which they appeared in the article?			
6. Did you keep the author's meaning the same?			
7. Did you use your own words?			
8. Did you use citation expressions to refer to the author's ideas?			

Unit 6: Active Tasks

1. Complete each Active Task.
2. Write the date you completed the task.
3. Write down the people you spoke to, the information you gathered, or the Internet addresses where you found information.
4. Write down your personal thoughts about the experience.

Lesson	Active Task	Action Date	People I Spoke To	Information I Gathered	Personal Thoughts
1	Ask your family and friends what they think your best skills are.				
2	Talk to three different people about their jobs. Ask them what their job titles are and what their responsibilities are.				
3	Look in the paper or on the Internet for a job that interests you and find out as much information as you can. Share your findings with the class.				

Unit 6
Active Task Checklist

Name: _____

Date: _____

Lesson	Active Task	Action Date	People I Spoke To	Information I Gathered	Personal Thoughts
3	Think of a company or business you have heard of and do some research on it. Find information in the library or on the Internet. Share your findings with the class.				
5	Go to the library or use the Internet to find tips on how to write your resume. Type your resume.				

Skills and Interests

• careful with details	• hard-working	• responsible
• customer service oriented	• a quick learner	• self-motivated
• dependable	• open-minded	• willing to accept responsibility
• efficient	• organized	• good under pressure
• flexible	• patient	• great with people
• good with numbers	• a problem solver	• a team player
	• reliable	

A. Complete each statement with a skill from the list above. There may be more than one possible answer.

1. A person who is _____ would be a good accountant.
2. A food server is usually _____.
3. A person who is _____ would make a great mechanic.
4. If you are _____, you could probably handle any job.
5. House cleaners should be _____.
6. An assembler is someone who is _____.
7. An athletic coach must be _____.
8. If you own your own business, you are most likely _____.
9. My strongest skill is that I am _____.
10. My weakest skill is that I am not _____.

B. Write your own statements like the ones above using the following words.

open-minded: _____

_____

flexible: _____

_____

willing to accept responsibility: _____

_____

Adjective Clauses

A. Remember that adjective clauses give more information about the subject. Study the information below.

Restrictive adjective clause: the extra information is necessary to understand the sentence

> The man is my brother-in-law. (which man?)
> The man *who owns his own business* is my brother-in-law.
>
> I quit the job. (which job?)
> I quit the job *that I used to have.*

Non-restrictive adjective clause: the extra information is not necessary to understand the sentence

> My brother-in-law, *who owns his own business*, works very hard.
> I quit my job, *which I never really liked anyway.*

Reminder: Use commas with non-restrictive adjective clauses but no commas for restrictive ones.

B. With a partner, make sentences using adjective clauses with the information about jobs in your book on page 103. Look at the examples below.

> Student A: A mechanic is good at fixing automobiles.
> Student B: The mechanic, *who is good at fixing automobiles,* now owns his own business.
>
> Student B: A busser clears and cleans tables in a restaurant.
> Student A: The busser clears and cleans tables in a restaurant *that is near his house.*

Student A: _____

Student B: _____

Student B: _____

Student A: _____

Name: _____

Date: _____

C. Combine the two sentences using an adjective clause.

1. My mother works for a clothing company. She loves the clothing company.

   _____

   _____

2. The architect got a bonus. The architect designs commercial buildings.

   _____

   _____

3. Maria decided to start her own business. Maria worked for someone else cleaning houses.

   _____

   _____

4. Linh asked her boss for a raise. Linh works as an assembler for a computer company.

   _____

   _____

5. Bahereh just got a new job as a food server. Bahereh moved here from Iran.

   _____

   _____

Name: _____

Date: _____

Job Search

A. Below is a job that appeared in the newspaper. Read the ad and complete the table below with the information you find.

> **Cashier needed!** Bianchi's Bagels, New York City-10th Ave Collect money, count money, talk to customers, use a cash register. Must be good with money, friendly, fast learner. Part-time/evenings 8.50/hour. Call Heidi (212) 555-9761.

Job Title	
Job Location	
Job Duties	
Necessary Qualifications	
Hours	
Salary	
Contact	
Phone	

1. Would you like to apply for this job? Why or why not?

_____

_____

2. Is there information missing from the ad that you would like to know? Write three questions below.

a. _____

b. _____

c. _____

B. Below is some information about Bianchi's Bagels. Read the information and answer the questions that follow.

Bianchi's Bagels
Founded: 1985
Number of stores: 50
Locations: New York, New Jersey, Maryland, Maine, North Carolina, South Carolina, Florida
Number of employees: 200
Company Mission: To provide fresh, hot, delicious bagels!

1. How many employees work for Bianchi's Bagels? _____

2. How many states will you find these bagel shops in? _____

3. How many years has this company been around? _____

4. What else would you like to know about this company?

_____

_____

_____

_____

Past Perfect

Write the correct form of the simple past or past perfect verb in the sentences below.

1. I _____ (work) for that company for 20 years before I _____ (get) this present job.

2. Morteza _____ (study) medicine at the university after he _____ (volunteer) in a family clinic for 5 years.

3. Ali _____ (meet) with her boss before she _____ (decide) to ask for a raise.

4. She finally _____ (find) a job after she _____ (look) for two months.

5. They finally _____ (finish) their project after they _____ (stay) up for 24 hours working on it.

6. Eric _____ (write) 5 resumes before he _____ (come) up with the perfect one.

7. Before Judy _____ (decide) to stay home and be a mom, she had _____ (teach) home economics to junior high school students.

8. After Kasia and Dave _____ (work) for 15 years as lawyers, they _____ (decide) to quit and join the Peace Corps.

Name: _____
Date: _____

Write a Resume

A. Interview a partner about his or her education, job experience, and special skills, and fill out the resume form below.

_____ (name)
_____ (address)
_____ (address)
_____ (phone)
_____ (email or alternate phone)

EDUCATION
_____

_____
_____

_____

_____

EXPERIENCE
_____

_____
_____

_____

_____
_____

SPECIAL SKILLS
_____
_____
_____

HOBBIES
_____

REFERENCES   _____ (name)   _____ (name)
                _____ (phone)   _____ (phone)

B. Have your partner look over the form. How does it look?

.

Name: _____

Date: _____

Write a Cover Letter

Imagine that your teacher is hiring a student to be his or her assistant in class and you would like to apply for the job. With your class, discuss what your teacher is looking for in an assistant and what sort of information should go in your cover letter. Write your cover letter on the lines below.

Name: _____
Date: _____

Interviews

A. Listen to the following job interviews. You will only hear a portion of each interview. Rate each interview according to what you hear. Circle your response.

Interview #1

Voice level (volume)	Bad	Fair	Excellent
Self-confidence	Bad	Fair	Excellent
Willingness to volunteer information	Bad	Fair	Excellent
Appropriateness of responses to questions	Bad	Fair	Excellent
Ability to self-evaluate	Bad	Fair	Excellent

Interview #2

Voice level (volume)	Bad	Fair	Excellent
Self-confidence	Bad	Fair	Excellent
Willingness to volunteer information	Bad	Fair	Excellent
Appropriateness of responses to questions	Bad	Fair	Excellent
Ability to self-evaluate	Bad	Fair	Excellent

Interview #3

Voice level (volume)	Bad	Fair	Excellent
Self-confidence	Bad	Fair	Excellent
Willingness to volunteer information	Bad	Fair	Excellent
Appropriateness of responses to questions	Bad	Fair	Excellent
Ability to self-evaluate	Bad	Fair	Excellent

Interview #4

Voice level (volume)	Bad	Fair	Excellent
Self-confidence	Bad	Fair	Excellent
Willingness to volunteer information	Bad	Fair	Excellent
Appropriateness of responses to questions	Bad	Fair	Excellent
Ability to self-evaluate	Bad	Fair	Excellent

B. Discuss the following questions.

1. Which person would you most like to hire? Why?

2. Which person would you never hire? Why not?

3. What are some good interview skills that you heard?

4. What are some bad interview skills that you heard?

Thank-You Letter

A. Read the thank-you letter that Ranjit wrote to Ms. Hawkins after his interview.

859 East 44th Street #16
New York, NY 10017

July 5, 2003

Ms. Jane Hawkins, Director
Trizon Electronics
497 West 67th Street, Fifth Floor
New York, NY 10017

Dear Ms. Hawkins:

I would like to personally thank you for the opportunity to interview for the computer technician position. I enjoyed meeting you and learning more about Trizon Electronics and all of your upcoming projects. I was especially impressed with your commitment to customer satisfaction and the initiative that your employees take to make that satisfaction a reality.

I believe that my education in India and my English class in the United States would make me a valuable employee and a strong addition to your team. Moreover, my experience at Global Concepts and CompuBuild, two New York-based companies, have really increased my knowledge of the computer market in the United States.

I look forward to hearing from you soon. Please call me if I can provide you with any more information or answer any additional questions you might have.

Sincerely,

Ranjit Ghosh
Ranjit Ghosh

B. Answer the following questions with a partner.
1. Why is Ranjit writing the letter?
2. What is the purpose of the ….first paragraph? ….the second? ….the third?
3. Why is it a good idea to write a thank-you letter after an interview?

Name: _____

Date: _____

C. Imagine you applied for a job that you are qualified for.

1. What is the job title?   _____

2. What is the name of the company? _____

3. Whom did you interview with?   _____

4. Why do you like the company?   _____

_____

_____

_____

_____

5. Why would you be a good employee for that company?

_____

_____

_____

_____

_____

D. On a separate piece of paper, write a cover letter to the person that you interviewed with. Use the information you wrote above and follow the format and style of the letter on the previous page.

Name: _____
Date: _____

Unit 7: Active Tasks

1. Complete each Active Task.
2. Write the date you completed the task.
3. Write down the people you spoke to, the information you gathered, or the Internet addresses where you found information.
4. Write down your personal thoughts about the experience.

Lesson	Active Task	Action Date	People I Spoke To	Information I Gathered	Personal Thoughts
6	Find a friend or family member and rehearse asking for a raise.				
6	Go to the library or look on the Internet to find tips on how to ask for a raise. Tell your class what you found out.				

Appropriate Classroom Behavior

A. In your book, you discussed appropriate workplace behavior. The same applies to the classroom. With a group, complete the table below with appropriate and inappropriate classroom behavior.

Appropriate Classroom Behavior	Inappropriate Classroom Behavior
Coming to class on time.	*Talking while the teacher is talking.*

B. Share your lists with the class. Can you add some behaviors to your list above that other groups mentioned?

C. Based on your list of appropriate and inappropriate classroom behavior, come up with a list of ten class rules that could be posted in your classroom.

Our Classroom Rules

1. **Come to class on time.**

2.

3.

4.

5.

6.

7.

8.

9.

10.

Name: _____
Date: _____

Passive Voice

Choose one of the words in the box below that best fits in each sentence and write the passive form of the verb on the lines provided.

build	repair
finalize	replace
find	send
give	steal
organize	write

1. Our new office building _____ two years ago.

2. Some paper towels _____ out of the supply room.

3. The retired doctor _____ by a young doctor, fresh out of medical school.

4. The Employee of the Year award _____ out at the end of the year luncheon.

5. Someone's purse _____ behind the tables in the employee lunch room.

6. The final report _____ solely by our team leader.

7. The stock room _____ by the maintenance crew before they left for the day.

8. The business trip plans _____ by our travel agent two weeks ago.

9. The boxes _____ last week. I don't know why they aren't here yet.

10. The old copy machine _____ for the last time. It's time to get a new one.

Name: _____
Date: _____

Active or Passive?

A. Decide if each statement below is written in active or passive voice. Write active or passive on the line. Then rewrite the sentence in the other voice.

1. The repairperson fixed the washing machine.

_____

_____

2. The employees were given bonuses this year by their boss.

_____

_____

3. Those papers were filed by the file clerk.

_____

_____

4. The Director of Human Resources gave a seminar on retirement options.

_____

_____

5. The construction workers filed a complaint because of unsafe working conditions.

_____

_____

6. The employees were informed of their new work schedule by their manager.

_____

_____

Name: _____

Date: _____

Finding a Solution

A. Listen to the conversation between an employee and his supervisor.

B. With a group, answer the following questions.

1. Did the employee try to solve the problem himself? _____ If yes, how?
_____

2. Did the employee ask a co-worker for help? _____ If yes, what happened?
_____
_____

3. Did the employee go to see the supervisor? _____

4. Did he politely get the supervisor's attention? _____

5. Did he clearly state the problem? _____ What is the problem? How did it happen? Who is involved?
_____
_____
_____
_____

6. Did the employee offer a solution or ask for a solution? _____

7. What do you think a good solution to this problem might be?
_____
_____
_____

C. Now listen to the entire conversation. What was the solution?

_____
_____

Did the employee clarify the solution be repeating it back to his supervisor? _____

Tag Questions

Complete each statement with the correct tag question.

1. They have never applied for this type of job, _____ ?

2. Kelsey works in marketing, _____ ?

3. The management team always has lunch at the Rooftop Grill, _____ ?

4. That customer wasn't very polite, _____ ?

5. She is living close to work, _____ ?

6. Shawn isn't going to work overtime tonight, _____ ?

7. Their company had to shut down last week, _____ ?

8. The president and CEO will be speaking at today's lunch, _____ ?

9. The new driver had never driven a truck before, _____ ?

10. We won't finish these reports in time, _____ ?

11. The office closes at 5pm, _____ ?

12. That outfit isn't appropriate for the workplace, _____ ?

13. Our new computers are networked, _____ ?

14. The handbook states that we get two weeks of vacation, _____ ?

15. They didn't get the shipment out on time, _____ ?

Ethical Dilemma

A. Read about Indira's dilemma.

My name is Indira and I am a part-time employee for a community college district. I am a test proctor, and I help out with the testing of new ESL students. My job is to administer the tests, score the tests, and then type the results on the computer. I really like my job because I like working with students and helping them find the right class.

Everything was going along fine until I noticed some of my co-workers taking advantage of the system. First of all, they finish their work really quickly and then take really long breaks at the coffee shop without clocking out. Second, they all cover for each other. For example, if one of them is going to be late or doesn't feel like coming in, another one will clock in for that person and then do his or her work. This really bothers me because I work so hard when I'm at work and I hate to see other people taking advantage of the system.

We have a supervisor, Julio, who schedules us and manages our work and I decided to tell him how I felt. I found out that he is one of them. He told me I wasn't being a team player and that I should go along with what everyone else does. I told him I didn't think that was the right thing to do.

I have a feeling I've gotten myself into a bad situation. The other day, his supervisor, Lilia, called me into her office and said that she had noticed a lot of mistakes in my work. I didn't know what she was talking about but when she showed me my testing reports, I could see that the actual test scores and what I had inputted into the computer didn't match. I told her I would be more careful. Now, every night before I leave my office, I double check all my numbers to make sure they match up.

But a week later, Lilia called me into her office again and said they were having the same problem with my reports. I can't understand what is happening. The only thing I can think of is that Julio is changing my reports to make me look bad. I think he's upset and worried that I might tell Lilia about the other employees' behavior. I don't know what to do. I really need this job. I want to talk to Lilia but I'm the new employee and I feel like it's my word against theirs.

Name: _____
Date: _____

B. With a group, discuss Indira's problem. Go through the steps for making an ethical decision.

1. Identify the issue or problem. _____
_____
_____

2. List the facts most relevant to Indira's decision.
_____
_____
_____
_____
_____
_____

3. Identify how people might be affected by Indira's decision and how.

Julio: _____
Lilia: _____
Other employees: _____

4. Explain what each person would want her to do about the situation.

Julio: _____
Lilia: _____
Other employees: _____

5. List three different decisions Indira could make and what the outcome of each decision might be.

Decision 1: _____
Decision 2: _____
Decision 3: _____

6. Decide what she should do: _____
_____
_____

Name: _____
Date: _____

Asking for a Raise

How did Nabil do with following the steps for asking for a raise? Reread Nabil's story on page 134 of your student book and complete the chart below.

HOW TO ASK FOR A RAISE	What did Nabil do?
1. Be a star performer.	
2. Research.	
3. Focus on your contributions to the company.	
4. Be informed.	
5. Timing is everything	
6. Do your homework.	
7. Rehearse.	
8. Be a professional.	
9. Cover your bases.	
10. Don't take no for an answer.	

Name: _____

Date: _____

Ask for a Raise – It's Your Turn

A. How would you ask for a raise at your job? (If you are a homemaker or a student, imagine you get paid for your work and you want a raise.) Make notes in the chart below about what you would do.

HOW TO ASK FOR A RAISE	What would you do?
1. Be a star performer.	
2. Research.	
3. Focus on your contributions to the company.	
4. Be informed.	
5. Timing is everything	
6. Do your homework.	
7. Rehearse.	
8. Be a professional.	
9. Cover your bases.	
10. Don't take no for an answer.	

B. Share your notes with a partner. Did your partner give you any good ideas?

Heinle © 2002
Stand Out 4 Activity Bank

Writing a Letter Asking for a Raise – Editing Checklist

A. Write a letter asking for a raise.

B. Use the checklist below to edit your letter. If you marked *No*, then go back to your letter and fix it. Put a check in the *Fixed* box.

	Yes	No	Fixed
1. Did you write the date at the top of your letter?			
2. Did you thank your supervisor for reading the letter?			
3. Did you include a greeting?			
4. Did you state the reason for writing your letter?			
5. Did you tell your supervisor how long you've been working for the company?			
6. Did you tell your supervisor what your job is?			
7. Did you tell your supervisor how your job has changed since you've been there?			
8. Did you tell your supervisor what you have done to help the company?			
9. Did you close your letter?			
10. Did you print your name and sign your letter?			

Name: _____

Date: _____

Unit 8: Active Tasks

1. Complete each Active Task.
2. Write the date you completed the task.
3. Write down the people you spoke to, the information you gathered, or the Internet addresses where you found information.
4. Write down your personal thoughts about the experience.

Lesson	Active Task	Action Date	People I Spoke To	Information I Gathered	Personal Thoughts
1	Talk to a friend or family member about civic responsibility.				
2	Go to the DMV and pick up a driver's handbook and a driver's license application.				
7	Look in the newspaper or on the Internet to find who is mayor or who is running for mayor in your town or city. What issues are they concerned about? What problems do they want to solve?				

Name: _____

Date: _____

Civic Responsibility

A. Create a matching activity by writing definitions in your own words for each of the words in the first column. Write the definitions in the second column, but don't write them directly across from the words. (Mix them up.)

1. car registration	
2. driver's license	
3. jury summons	
4. taxes	
5. traffic ticket	
6. voter registration	

B. Now give your paper to a partner and see if he or she can complete the matching activity by drawing lines from the words to the definitions.

C. Answer the following questions about yourself. Then interview your partner with the same questions. Put a check in the correct column.

	YOU		YOUR PARTNER	
	YES	NO	YES	NO
1. Do you drive a car?				
If yes, is your car registered?				
2. Do you have a driver's license?				
3. Have you ever received a jury summons?				
If yes, did you fill it out and send it back?				
4. Have you ever gotten a traffic ticket?				
5. Do you pay taxes?				
6. Are you registered to vote?				

D. Compare your experiences with your partner.

Name: _____

Date: _____

Driving Safety

A. What are some important safety laws you should obey while driving a motor vehicle? Make a list with a group.

_____

_____

_____

_____

B. Read the following information on driving safety.

Alcohol

It is against the law to drive while under the influence of alcohol and you could get a ticket for DUI (Driving Under the Influence) if your BAC (blood alcohol level) is .08 or higher. Penalties include fines, community service, probation, license revocation, DUI school, and possibly imprisonment. The more convictions you have, the stronger the punishment will be.

Safety Belts and Restraints

Any person 6 years of age or older must wear a seat belt while seated in any position of a motor vehicle. The driver of the car is responsible for any passenger in the car not wearing seat belts.

Children and infants up to three years of age must be secured in a child restraint device (car seat) that has been federally approved and crash tested. Children ages four to five can be secured in a car seat or a seat belt.

Speed Limits

Speed limits give the top speed you may drive in a motor vehicle and the limits vary depending where you are driving: 30 MPH (miles per hour) in business and residential areas, 55 MPH on most roads and highways, and 70 MPH on rural interstates. You should always drive at a safe speed that allows you to stay in control of your vehicle.

Law Enforcement and Traffic Accidents

When a police officer pulls you over, pull over to an area where you will not be blocking traffic. Turn off your engine and reduce your headlights if it is night time. Wait for the police officer to give you instructions and follow his or her instructions carefully. It is a good idea to put your hands on the steering wheel so the officer doesn't think you are doing anything suspicious.

If you are involved in a crash while driving, follow these steps:
1. Stop to help anyone who has been injured and give your personal and insurance information to others involved.
2. Report the crash to the Police Department.
3. Move your car out of the way of traffic.
4. Appear in court to explain what happened.

Automobile Insurance

All drivers must have automobile insurance to cover themselves and others who may be injured in automobile accident. You must continue to have car insurance for any car that is registered in your name, even if you are no longer driving it. You are still financially responsible for the car.

Source: California Department of Motor Vehicles http://www.dmv.ca.gov

Name: _____

Date: _____

C. Safety laws vary from state to state. What does the reading say about each of the following safety laws? Write the answers in the chart. Is the same true in your state? Find out the laws in your state for these issues. (Hint: search on the Internet, talk to people who have their driver's licenses, visit the motor vehicle office in your city, etc.)

	The reading says.....	Your state law says......
At what age must people wear seatbelts?		
At what age must children be put in a child restraint?		
Who needs insurance?		
What is the speed limit in a residential area? On most highways?		
At what BAC will you get a DUI?		
What should you do if you are in a traffic accident?		

Name: _____
Date: _____

Jury Summons Information

A. Discuss these questions with your class. Use the Internet or go to your library to check your answers.

1. How do they get my name to send me a jury summons?

2. How long does jury duty usually last?

3. Can I postpone jury duty?

4. Can I be excused from jury duty?

5. Will I be paid for jury service?

B. Answer the following questions.

1. Is it possible for <u>you</u> to get a jury summons in the mail? Why or why not?
_____
_____

2. Are you qualified to serve as a juror? Why or why not?
_____
_____

3. Would you like to serve on jury duty? Why or why not?
_____
_____
_____
_____
_____
_____

Name: _____

Date: _____

Tax Form Calculations

A. Below are partial tax forms for 4 different people. Complete the calculations.

Person A

Income	7. Wages, salaries, tips, etc. Attach forms(s) W-2	7	25, 687.00
	8. Taxable interest	8	12.42
	9. Add the amounts for lines 7 and 8. This is your total income.	9	_____

Tax and Credits	10. Amount from line 9	10	_____
Standard Deduction	11. Enter your standard deduction from the left.	11	4,400.00
Single: $4,400	12. Subtract line 11 from line 10	12	_____
Head of Household: $6, 450	13. If line 10 is less than $96, 700, multiply $2,800	13	_____
Married Filing Jointly or	by the total number of exemptions claimed on line 6d		
Qualifying Widow(er):	14. Subtract line 13 from line 12. This is your	14	_____
$7,350	taxable income. If line 13 is more than line 12, enter		
Married Filing Separately:	0.		
$3,675	15. Tax (see tax schedule)	15	_____

Person B

Income	7. Wages, salaries, tips, etc. Attach forms(s) W-2	7	85, 274.78
	8. Taxable interest	8	125.35
	9. Add the amounts for lines 7 and 8. This is your total income.	9	_____

Tax and Credits	10. Amount from line 9	10	_____
Standard Deduction	11. Enter your standard deduction from the left.	11	3,675.00
Single: $4,400	12. Subtract line 11 from line 10	12	_____
Head of Household: $6, 450	13. If line 10 is less than $96, 700, multiply $2,800	13	_____
Married Filing Jointly or	by the total number of exemptions claimed on line 6d		
Qualifying Widow(er):	14. Subtract line 13 from line 12. This is your	14	_____
$7,350	taxable income. If line 13 is more than line 12, enter		
Married Filing Separately:	0.		
$3,675	15. Tax (see tax schedule)	15	_____

Name: _____

Date: _____

Person C

Income	7. Wages, salaries, tips, etc. Attach forms(s) W-2	7	37,927.02
	8. Taxable interest	8	24.98
	9. Add the amounts for lines 7 and 8. This is your total income.	9	_____

Tax and Credits	10. Amount from line 9	10	
Standard Deduction	11. Enter your standard deduction from the left.	11	7,350.00
Single: $4,400	12. Subtract line 11 from line 10	12	_____
Head of Household: $6,450	13. If line 10 is less than $96,700, multiply $2,800 by the total number of exemptions claimed on line 6d	13	_____
Married Filing Jointly or Qualifying Widow(er): $7,350	14. Subtract line 13 from line 12. This is your taxable income. If line 13 is more than line 12, enter 0.	14	_____
Married Filing Separately: $3,675	15. Tax (see tax schedule)	15	_____

Person D

Income	7. Wages, salaries, tips, etc. Attach forms(s) W-2	7	125,456.09
	8. Taxable interest	8	578.00
	9. Add the amounts for lines 7 and 8. This is your total income.	9	_____

Tax and Credits	10. Amount from line 9	10	
Standard Deduction	11. Enter your standard deduction from the left.	11	6,450.00
Single: $4,400	12. Subtract line 11 from line 10	12	_____
Head of Household: $6,450	13. If line 10 is less than $96,700, multiply $2,800 by the total number of exemptions claimed on line 6d	13	_____
Married Filing Jointly or Qualifying Widow(er): $7,350	14. Subtract line 13 from line 12. This is your taxable income. If line 13 is more than line 12, enter 0.	14	_____
Married Filing Separately: $3,675	15. Tax (see tax schedule)	15	_____

B. See if you got the same answers as the people sitting next to you.

C. Go over the answers with your class.

Source: Tax form information from Internal Revenue Service, Department of the Treasury

Name: _____

Date: _____

Register to Vote

A. Answer the questions.

Have you ever voted in an election in your country? _____ If so, when? _____

Have you ever voted in an election in the United States? _____ If so, when? _____

B. Read about voting eligibility.

To be eligible to register to vote in a federal election you must*:

    be a United States Citizen
    be 18 years of age on or before the day of the election
    be a resident of the one of the states in the United States
    not be in prison or on parole for the conviction of a felony

*Requirements vary by state.

felony-n. a serious crime, such as murder

C. Are you eligible to vote in a federal election? Check *yes* or *no* for each statement below.

	YES	NO
I am a U.S. citizen.		
I am 18 years old.		
I will be 18 years old by the next election. (Ask your teacher when this is.)		
I am a resident of the United States.		
I am **not** in prison for the conviction of a felony.		
I am **not** on parole for the conviction of a felony.		

D. If you are eligible to vote, get a voter registration card for your state and register today!

Name: _____
Date: _____

Editing Checklist
Formatting, Mechanics, Sentence Types, Transitions

Look at your paragraph and answer the following questions. If you marked no, try to fix your mistake.

Formatting

Did you put your title in the center of your paper?   yes o   no o

Did you leave a space between the title and the first sentence of the paragraph?   yes o   no o

Did you indent the first sentence of your paragraph?   yes o   no o

Did you leave margins on the right side of your paper?   yes o   no o

Did you leave margins on the left side of your paper?   yes o   no o

Sentence Types

Does your paragraph have a topic sentence?   yes o   no o

Is your topic sentence the main idea of your paper?   yes o   no o

Does your paragraph have at least 2 support sentences?   yes o   no o

Does your paragraph have a conclusion sentence?   yes o   no o

Mechanics

Does every sentence begin with a capital letter?   yes o   no o

Does every sentence end with a punctuation mark?   yes o   no o

Is every word spelled correctly?   yes o   no o

Do all your subjects and verbs agree?   yes o   no o

Transitions

Did you use transitions to connect your sentences?   yes o   no o

Name: _____
Date: _____

Peer Editing Checklist
Formatting, Mechanics, Sentence Types, Transitions

Look at your partner's paragraph and answer the following questions.

<u>Formatting</u>
Is the title in the center of the paper?   yes o   no o

Is there a space between the title and the first sentence of the paragraph?   yes o   no o

Did the author indent the first sentence of the paragraph?   yes o   no o

Are there margins on the right side of the paper?   yes o   no o

Are there margins on the left side of the paper?   yes o   no o

<u>Sentence Types</u>
Does the paragraph have a topic sentence?   yes o   no o

Is the topic sentence the main idea of the paper?   yes o   no o

Does the paragraph have at least 2 support sentences?   yes o   no o

Does the paragraph have a conclusion sentence?   yes o   no o

<u>Mechanics</u>
Does every sentence begin with a capital letter?   yes o   no o

Does every sentence end with a punctuation mark?   yes o   no o

Is every word spelled correctly?   yes o   no o

Do all the subjects and verbs agree?   yes o   no o

<u>Transitions</u>
Are there transitions to connect the sentences?   yes o   no o

Name:
Date:

Writing a Letter to a Community Official – Editing Checklist

A. Write a letter to a community official about a problem in your community.

B. Use the checklist below to edit your letter. If you marked *No*, then go back to your letter and fix it. Put a check in the *Fixed* box.

	Yes	No	Fixed
1. Did you write the date at the top of your letter?			
2. Did you write your name and address at the top of the letter?			
3. Did you include the official's name and address?			
4. Did you include a greeting?			
5. Did you state the problem?			
6. Did you give facts or anecdotes about the problem?			
7. Did you give some suggested solutions?			
8. Did you thank the person for taking the time to read your letter?			
9. Did you close your letter?			
10. Did you print your name and sign your letter?			

Name: _____

Date: _____

Passive Modals

Look at each of the statements by Antonio Juliana and Gary Hurt. Rewrite each statement using passive modals with one of the expressions in the box.

believes that	insists that
says that	demands that
thinks that	points out that

1. Antonio Juliana wants to clean up the streets.

_____

2. Antonio Juliana hopes to lower tuition fees.

_____

3. Antonio Juliana intends to improve public transportation.

_____

4. Antonio Juliana wants to decrease gang violence.

_____

5. Antonio Juliana wants to get kids off the streets.

_____

6. Antonio Juliana wants to help the homeless people.

_____

7. Antonio Juliana plans to increase environmental awareness.

_____

8. Gary Hurt promises to clean up the beaches.

_____

9. Gary Hurt hopes to improve the transportation system.

_____

10. Gary Hurt intends to build safe parks for children.

_____

Name: _____
Date: _____

Sample Ballot

Directions: Please vote for ONE of the following by putting a check in the box next to his or her name.

	My Vote
Gary Hurt	
Antonio Juliana	
Kwan Tan	

Stand Out CASAS Style Test Answer Sheet

Student Last Name   First   Middle

Instructor Name

Marking Answers

Use number 2 pencil	**Right**
Do NOT use pen	(A) (B) ● (D)
Make dark marks that fill out completely	**Wrong**
Erase completely any answers you change	(A) (B̶) (C) (D) (A) (B) (C) (⊖)

Student Identification

①	⓪	⓪	⓪	⓪	⓪	⓪	⓪	⓪
②	②	②	②	②	②	②	②	②
③	③	③	③	③	③	③	③	③
④	④	④	④	④	④	④	④	④
⑤	⑤	⑤	⑤	⑤	⑤	⑤	⑤	⑤
⑥	⑥	⑥	⑥	⑥	⑥	⑥	⑥	⑥
⑦	⑦	⑦	⑦	⑦	⑦	⑦	⑦	⑦
⑧	⑧	⑧	⑧	⑧	⑧	⑧	⑧	⑧
⑨	⑨	⑨	⑨	⑨	⑨	⑨	⑨	⑨

Test Date

Month		Day		Year
Jan	①	⓪	⓪	200 ⓪
Feb	②	①	①	200 ①
Mar	③	②	②	200 ②
Apr	④	③	③	200 ③
May	⑤		④	200 ④
Jun	⑥		⑤	200 ⑤
Jul	⑦		⑥	200 ⑥
Aug	⑧		⑦	200 ⑦
Sept	⑨		⑧	200 ⑧
Oct	⑩		⑨	200 ⑨
Nov	⑪			
Dec	⑫			

Test Answers

1	(A)	(B)	(C)	(D)
2	(A)	(B)	(C)	(D)
3	(A)	(B)	(C)	(D)
4	(A)	(B)	(C)	(D)
5	(A)	(B)	(C)	(D)
6	(A)	(B)	(C)	(D)
7	(A)	(B)	(C)	(D)
8	(A)	(B)	(C)	(D)
9	(A)	(B)	(C)	(D)
10	(A)	(B)	(C)	(D)
11	(A)	(B)	(C)	(D)
12	(A)	(B)	(C)	(D)
13	(A)	(B)	(C)	(D)
14	(A)	(B)	(C)	(D)
15	(A)	(B)	(C)	(D)
16	(A)	(B)	(C)	(D)
17	(A)	(B)	(C)	(D)
18	(A)	(B)	(C)	(D)
19	(A)	(B)	(C)	(D)
20	(A)	(B)	(C)	(D)
21	(A)	(B)	(C)	(D)
22	(A)	(B)	(C)	(D)
23	(A)	(B)	(C)	(D)
24	(A)	(B)	(C)	(D)
25	(A)	(B)	(C)	(D)
26	(A)	(B)	(C)	(D)
27	(A)	(B)	(C)	(D)
28	(A)	(B)	(C)	(D)
29	(A)	(B)	(C)	(D)
30	(A)	(B)	(C)	(D)
31	(A)	(B)	(C)	(D)
32	(A)	(B)	(C)	(D)
33	(A)	(B)	(C)	(D)
34	(A)	(B)	(C)	(D)
35	(A)	(B)	(C)	(D)
36	(A)	(B)	(C)	(D)
37	(A)	(B)	(C)	(D)
38	(A)	(B)	(C)	(D)
39	(A)	(B)	(C)	(D)
40	(A)	(B)	(C)	(D)
41	(A)	(B)	(C)	(D)
42	(A)	(B)	(C)	(D)
43	(A)	(B)	(C)	(D)
44	(A)	(B)	(C)	(D)
45	(A)	(B)	(C)	(D)
46	(A)	(B)	(C)	(D)
47	(A)	(B)	(C)	(D)
48	(A)	(B)	(C)	(D)
49	(A)	(B)	(C)	(D)
50	(A)	(B)	(C)	(D)

Stand Out CASAS Style Test Answer Sheet

Student Last Name	First	Middle

Instructor Name

Marking Answers

Use number 2 pencil	**Right**
Do NOT use pen	Ⓐ Ⓑ ● Ⓓ
Make dark marks that fill out completely	**Wrong**
Erase completely any answers you change	Ⓐ Ⓑ̸ Ⓒ Ⓓ Ⓐ Ⓑ Ⓒ ●

Student Identification

(1) (0) (0) (0) (0) (0) (0) (0) (0)
(2) (2) (2) (2) (2) (2) (2) (2) (2)
(3) (3) (3) (3) (3) (3) (3) (3) (3)
(4) (4) (4) (4) (4) (4) (4) (4) (4)
(5) (5) (5) (5) (5) (5) (5) (5) (5)
(6) (6) (6) (6) (6) (6) (6) (6) (6)
(7) (7) (7) (7) (7) (7) (7) (7) (7)
(8) (8) (8) (8) (8) (8) (8) (8) (8)
(9) (9) (9) (9) (9) (9) (9) (9) (9)

Test Date

Month	Day		Year
Jan (1)	(0)	(0)	200 (0)
Feb (2)	(1)	(1)	200 (1)
Mar (3)	(2)	(2)	200 (2)
Apr (4)	(3)	(3)	200 (3)
May (5)		(4)	200 (4)
Jun (6)		(5)	200 (5)
Jul (7)		(6)	200 (6)
Aug (8)		(7)	200 (7)
Sept (9)		(8)	200 (8)
Oct (10)		(9)	200 (9)
Nov (11)			
Dec (12)			

Test Answers

1 Ⓐ Ⓑ Ⓒ Ⓓ
2 Ⓐ Ⓑ Ⓒ Ⓓ
3 Ⓐ Ⓑ Ⓒ Ⓓ
4 Ⓐ Ⓑ Ⓒ Ⓓ
5 Ⓐ Ⓑ Ⓒ Ⓓ
6 Ⓐ Ⓑ Ⓒ Ⓓ
7 Ⓐ Ⓑ Ⓒ Ⓓ
8 Ⓐ Ⓑ Ⓒ Ⓓ
9 Ⓐ Ⓑ Ⓒ Ⓓ
10 Ⓐ Ⓑ Ⓒ Ⓓ
11 Ⓐ Ⓑ Ⓒ Ⓓ
12 Ⓐ Ⓑ Ⓒ Ⓓ
13 Ⓐ Ⓑ Ⓒ Ⓓ
14 Ⓐ Ⓑ Ⓒ Ⓓ
15 Ⓐ Ⓑ Ⓒ Ⓓ
16 Ⓐ Ⓑ Ⓒ Ⓓ
17 Ⓐ Ⓑ Ⓒ Ⓓ
18 Ⓐ Ⓑ Ⓒ Ⓓ
19 Ⓐ Ⓑ Ⓒ Ⓓ
20 Ⓐ Ⓑ Ⓒ Ⓓ
21 Ⓐ Ⓑ Ⓒ Ⓓ
22 Ⓐ Ⓑ Ⓒ Ⓓ
23 Ⓐ Ⓑ Ⓒ Ⓓ
24 Ⓐ Ⓑ Ⓒ Ⓓ
25 Ⓐ Ⓑ Ⓒ Ⓓ
26 Ⓐ Ⓑ Ⓒ Ⓓ
27 Ⓐ Ⓑ Ⓒ Ⓓ
28 Ⓐ Ⓑ Ⓒ Ⓓ
29 Ⓐ Ⓑ Ⓒ Ⓓ
30 Ⓐ Ⓑ Ⓒ Ⓓ
31 Ⓐ Ⓑ Ⓒ Ⓓ
32 Ⓐ Ⓑ Ⓒ Ⓓ
33 Ⓐ Ⓑ Ⓒ Ⓓ
34 Ⓐ Ⓑ Ⓒ Ⓓ
35 Ⓐ Ⓑ Ⓒ Ⓓ
36 Ⓐ Ⓑ Ⓒ Ⓓ
37 Ⓐ Ⓑ Ⓒ Ⓓ
38 Ⓐ Ⓑ Ⓒ Ⓓ
39 Ⓐ Ⓑ Ⓒ Ⓓ
40 Ⓐ Ⓑ Ⓒ Ⓓ
41 Ⓐ Ⓑ Ⓒ Ⓓ
42 Ⓐ Ⓑ Ⓒ Ⓓ
43 Ⓐ Ⓑ Ⓒ Ⓓ
44 Ⓐ Ⓑ Ⓒ Ⓓ
45 Ⓐ Ⓑ Ⓒ Ⓓ
46 Ⓐ Ⓑ Ⓒ Ⓓ
47 Ⓐ Ⓑ Ⓒ Ⓓ
48 Ⓐ Ⓑ Ⓒ Ⓓ
49 Ⓐ Ⓑ Ⓒ Ⓓ
50 Ⓐ Ⓑ Ⓒ Ⓓ

Stand Out CASAS Style Test Answer Sheet

Student Last Name   First   Middle

Instructor Name

Test Answers

1	Ⓐ Ⓑ Ⓒ Ⓓ
2	Ⓐ Ⓑ Ⓒ Ⓓ
3	Ⓐ Ⓑ Ⓒ Ⓓ
4	Ⓐ Ⓑ Ⓒ Ⓓ
5	Ⓐ Ⓑ Ⓒ Ⓓ
6	Ⓐ Ⓑ Ⓒ Ⓓ
7	Ⓐ Ⓑ Ⓒ Ⓓ
8	Ⓐ Ⓑ Ⓒ Ⓓ
9	Ⓐ Ⓑ Ⓒ Ⓓ
10	Ⓐ Ⓑ Ⓒ Ⓓ
11	Ⓐ Ⓑ Ⓒ Ⓓ
12	Ⓐ Ⓑ Ⓒ Ⓓ
13	Ⓐ Ⓑ Ⓒ Ⓓ
14	Ⓐ Ⓑ Ⓒ Ⓓ
15	Ⓐ Ⓑ Ⓒ Ⓓ
16	Ⓐ Ⓑ Ⓒ Ⓓ
17	Ⓐ Ⓑ Ⓒ Ⓓ
18	Ⓐ Ⓑ Ⓒ Ⓓ
19	Ⓐ Ⓑ Ⓒ Ⓓ
20	Ⓐ Ⓑ Ⓒ Ⓓ
21	Ⓐ Ⓑ Ⓒ Ⓓ
22	Ⓐ Ⓑ Ⓒ Ⓓ
23	Ⓐ Ⓑ Ⓒ Ⓓ
24	Ⓐ Ⓑ Ⓒ Ⓓ
25	Ⓐ Ⓑ Ⓒ Ⓓ
26	Ⓐ Ⓑ Ⓒ Ⓓ
27	Ⓐ Ⓑ Ⓒ Ⓓ
28	Ⓐ Ⓑ Ⓒ Ⓓ
29	Ⓐ Ⓑ Ⓒ Ⓓ
30	Ⓐ Ⓑ Ⓒ Ⓓ
31	Ⓐ Ⓑ Ⓒ Ⓓ
32	Ⓐ Ⓑ Ⓒ Ⓓ
33	Ⓐ Ⓑ Ⓒ Ⓓ
34	Ⓐ Ⓑ Ⓒ Ⓓ
35	Ⓐ Ⓑ Ⓒ Ⓓ
36	Ⓐ Ⓑ Ⓒ Ⓓ
37	Ⓐ Ⓑ Ⓒ Ⓓ
38	Ⓐ Ⓑ Ⓒ Ⓓ
39	Ⓐ Ⓑ Ⓒ Ⓓ
40	Ⓐ Ⓑ Ⓒ Ⓓ
41	Ⓐ Ⓑ Ⓒ Ⓓ
42	Ⓐ Ⓑ Ⓒ Ⓓ
43	Ⓐ Ⓑ Ⓒ Ⓓ
44	Ⓐ Ⓑ Ⓒ Ⓓ
45	Ⓐ Ⓑ Ⓒ Ⓓ
46	Ⓐ Ⓑ Ⓒ Ⓓ
47	Ⓐ Ⓑ Ⓒ Ⓓ
48	Ⓐ Ⓑ Ⓒ Ⓓ
49	Ⓐ Ⓑ Ⓒ Ⓓ
50	Ⓐ Ⓑ Ⓒ Ⓓ

Marking Answers

Use number 2 pencil	**Right** Ⓐ Ⓑ ● Ⓓ
Do NOT use pen	
Make dark marks that fill out completely	**Wrong** Ⓐ ⊗ Ⓒ Ⓓ
Erase completely any answers you change	Ⓐ Ⓑ Ⓒ **Ⓓ**

Student Identification

①	⓪	⓪	⓪	⓪	⓪	⓪	⓪	⓪
②	②	②	②	②	②	②	②	②
③	③	③	③	③	③	③	③	③
④	④	④	④	④	④	④	④	④
⑤	⑤	⑤	⑤	⑤	⑤	⑤	⑤	⑤
⑥	⑥	⑥	⑥	⑥	⑥	⑥	⑥	⑥
⑦	⑦	⑦	⑦	⑦	⑦	⑦	⑦	⑦
⑧	⑧	⑧	⑧	⑧	⑧	⑧	⑧	⑧
⑨	⑨	⑨	⑨	⑨	⑨	⑨	⑨	⑨

Test Date

Month		Day		Year	
Jan	①	⓪	⓪	200	⓪
Feb	②	①	①	200	①
Mar	③	②	②	200	②
Apr	④	③	③	200	③
May	⑤		④	200	④
Jun	⑥		⑤	200	⑤
Jul	⑦		⑥	200	⑥
Aug	⑧		⑦	200	⑦
Sept	⑨		⑧	200	⑧
Oct	⑩		⑨	200	⑨
Nov	⑪				
Dec	⑫				

Stand Out CASAS Style Test Answer Sheet

Student Last Name   First   Middle

Instructor Name

Marking Answers

Use number 2 pencil	**Right**
Do NOT use pen	Ⓐ Ⓑ ● Ⓓ
Make dark marks that fill out completely	**Wrong**
Erase completely any answers you change	Ⓐ Ⓑ̶ Ⓒ Ⓓ Ⓐ Ⓑ Ⓒ **Ⓓ**

Test Answers

1 Ⓐ Ⓑ Ⓒ Ⓓ
2 Ⓐ Ⓑ Ⓒ Ⓓ
3 Ⓐ Ⓑ Ⓒ Ⓓ
4 Ⓐ Ⓑ Ⓒ Ⓓ
5 Ⓐ Ⓑ Ⓒ Ⓓ
6 Ⓐ Ⓑ Ⓒ Ⓓ
7 Ⓐ Ⓑ Ⓒ Ⓓ
8 Ⓐ Ⓑ Ⓒ Ⓓ
9 Ⓐ Ⓑ Ⓒ Ⓓ
10 Ⓐ Ⓑ Ⓒ Ⓓ
11 Ⓐ Ⓑ Ⓒ Ⓓ
12 Ⓐ Ⓑ Ⓒ Ⓓ
13 Ⓐ Ⓑ Ⓒ Ⓓ
14 Ⓐ Ⓑ Ⓒ Ⓓ
15 Ⓐ Ⓑ Ⓒ Ⓓ
16 Ⓐ Ⓑ Ⓒ Ⓓ
17 Ⓐ Ⓑ Ⓒ Ⓓ
18 Ⓐ Ⓑ Ⓒ Ⓓ
19 Ⓐ Ⓑ Ⓒ Ⓓ
20 Ⓐ Ⓑ Ⓒ Ⓓ
21 Ⓐ Ⓑ Ⓒ Ⓓ
22 Ⓐ Ⓑ Ⓒ Ⓓ
23 Ⓐ Ⓑ Ⓒ Ⓓ
24 Ⓐ Ⓑ Ⓒ Ⓓ
25 Ⓐ Ⓑ Ⓒ Ⓓ
26 Ⓐ Ⓑ Ⓒ Ⓓ
27 Ⓐ Ⓑ Ⓒ Ⓓ
28 Ⓐ Ⓑ Ⓒ Ⓓ
29 Ⓐ Ⓑ Ⓒ Ⓓ
30 Ⓐ Ⓑ Ⓒ Ⓓ
31 Ⓐ Ⓑ Ⓒ Ⓓ
32 Ⓐ Ⓑ Ⓒ Ⓓ
33 Ⓐ Ⓑ Ⓒ Ⓓ
34 Ⓐ Ⓑ Ⓒ Ⓓ
35 Ⓐ Ⓑ Ⓒ Ⓓ
36 Ⓐ Ⓑ Ⓒ Ⓓ
37 Ⓐ Ⓑ Ⓒ Ⓓ
38 Ⓐ Ⓑ Ⓒ Ⓓ
39 Ⓐ Ⓑ Ⓒ Ⓓ
40 Ⓐ Ⓑ Ⓒ Ⓓ
41 Ⓐ Ⓑ Ⓒ Ⓓ
42 Ⓐ Ⓑ Ⓒ Ⓓ
43 Ⓐ Ⓑ Ⓒ Ⓓ
44 Ⓐ Ⓑ Ⓒ Ⓓ
45 Ⓐ Ⓑ Ⓒ Ⓓ
46 Ⓐ Ⓑ Ⓒ Ⓓ
47 Ⓐ Ⓑ Ⓒ Ⓓ
48 Ⓐ Ⓑ Ⓒ Ⓓ
49 Ⓐ Ⓑ Ⓒ Ⓓ
50 Ⓐ Ⓑ Ⓒ Ⓓ

Student Identification

①	⓪	⓪	⓪	⓪	⓪	⓪	⓪	⓪
②	②	②	②	②	②	②	②	②
③	③	③	③	③	③	③	③	③
④	④	④	④	④	④	④	④	④
⑤	⑤	⑤	⑤	⑤	⑤	⑤	⑤	⑤
⑥	⑥	⑥	⑥	⑥	⑥	⑥	⑥	⑥
⑦	⑦	⑦	⑦	⑦	⑦	⑦	⑦	⑦
⑧	⑧	⑧	⑧	⑧	⑧	⑧	⑧	⑧
⑨	⑨	⑨	⑨	⑨	⑨	⑨	⑨	⑨

Test Date

Month	Day		Year
Jan ①	⓪	⓪	200 ⓪
Feb ②	①	①	200 ①
Mar ③	②	②	200 ②
Apr ④	③	③	200 ③
May ⑤		④	200 ④
Jun ⑥		⑤	200 ⑤
Jul ⑦		⑥	200 ⑥
Aug ⑧		⑦	200 ⑦
Sept ⑨		⑧	200 ⑧
Oct ⑩		⑨	200 ⑨
Nov ⑪			
Dec ⑫			

Stand Out CASAS Style Test Answer Sheet

Student Last Name   First   Middle

Instructor Name

Marking Answers

Use number 2 pencil	Right
Do NOT use pen	(A) (B) ● (D)
Make dark marks that fill out completely	Wrong
Erase completely any answers you change	(A) (⊗B) (C) (D) (A) (B) (C) (●D)

Student Identification

①	⓪	⓪	⓪	⓪	⓪	⓪	⓪	⓪
②	②	②	②	②	②	②	②	②
③	③	③	③	③	③	③	③	③
④	④	④	④	④	④	④	④	④
⑤	⑤	⑤	⑤	⑤	⑤	⑤	⑤	⑤
⑥	⑥	⑥	⑥	⑥	⑥	⑥	⑥	⑥
⑦	⑦	⑦	⑦	⑦	⑦	⑦	⑦	⑦
⑧	⑧	⑧	⑧	⑧	⑧	⑧	⑧	⑧
⑨	⑨	⑨	⑨	⑨	⑨	⑨	⑨	⑨

Test Date

Month		Day		Year	
Jan	①	⓪	⓪	200	⓪
Feb	②	①	①	200	①
Mar	③	②	②	200	②
Apr	④	③	③	200	③
May	⑤		④	200	④
Jun	⑥		⑤	200	⑤
Jul	⑦		⑥	200	⑥
Aug	⑧		⑦	200	⑦
Sept	⑨		⑧	200	⑧
Oct	⑩		⑨	200	⑨
Nov	⑪				
Dec	⑫				

Test Answers

1	(A)	(B)	(C)	(D)
2	(A)	(B)	(C)	(D)
3	(A)	(B)	(C)	(D)
4	(A)	(B)	(C)	(D)
5	(A)	(B)	(C)	(D)
6	(A)	(B)	(C)	(D)
7	(A)	(B)	(C)	(D)
8	(A)	(B)	(C)	(D)
9	(A)	(B)	(C)	(D)
10	(A)	(B)	(C)	(D)
11	(A)	(B)	(C)	(D)
12	(A)	(B)	(C)	(D)
13	(A)	(B)	(C)	(D)
14	(A)	(B)	(C)	(D)
15	(A)	(B)	(C)	(D)
16	(A)	(B)	(C)	(D)
17	(A)	(B)	(C)	(D)
18	(A)	(B)	(C)	(D)
19	(A)	(B)	(C)	(D)
20	(A)	(B)	(C)	(D)
21	(A)	(B)	(C)	(D)
22	(A)	(B)	(C)	(D)
23	(A)	(B)	(C)	(D)
24	(A)	(B)	(C)	(D)
25	(A)	(B)	(C)	(D)
26	(A)	(B)	(C)	(D)
27	(A)	(B)	(C)	(D)
28	(A)	(B)	(C)	(D)
29	(A)	(B)	(C)	(D)
30	(A)	(B)	(C)	(D)
31	(A)	(B)	(C)	(D)
32	(A)	(B)	(C)	(D)
33	(A)	(B)	(C)	(D)
34	(A)	(B)	(C)	(D)
35	(A)	(B)	(C)	(D)
36	(A)	(B)	(C)	(D)
37	(A)	(B)	(C)	(D)
38	(A)	(B)	(C)	(D)
39	(A)	(B)	(C)	(D)
40	(A)	(B)	(C)	(D)
41	(A)	(B)	(C)	(D)
42	(A)	(B)	(C)	(D)
43	(A)	(B)	(C)	(D)
44	(A)	(B)	(C)	(D)
45	(A)	(B)	(C)	(D)
46	(A)	(B)	(C)	(D)
47	(A)	(B)	(C)	(D)
48	(A)	(B)	(C)	(D)
49	(A)	(B)	(C)	(D)
50	(A)	(B)	(C)	(D)

Stand Out CASAS Style Test Answer Sheet

Student Last Name	First	Middle

Instructor Name

Marking Answers

Use number 2 pencil	Right
Do NOT use pen	Ⓐ Ⓑ ● Ⓓ
Make dark marks that fill out completely	Wrong
Erase completely any answers you change	Ⓐ ⊗ Ⓒ Ⓓ Ⓐ Ⓑ Ⓒ Ⓓ

Student Identification

①	⓪	⓪	⓪	⓪	⓪	⓪	⓪	⓪
②	②	②	②	②	②	②	②	②
③	③	③	③	③	③	③	③	③
④	④	④	④	④	④	④	④	④
⑤	⑤	⑤	⑤	⑤	⑤	⑤	⑤	⑤
⑥	⑥	⑥	⑥	⑥	⑥	⑥	⑥	⑥
⑦	⑦	⑦	⑦	⑦	⑦	⑦	⑦	⑦
⑧	⑧	⑧	⑧	⑧	⑧	⑧	⑧	⑧
⑨	⑨	⑨	⑨	⑨	⑨	⑨	⑨	⑨

Test Date

Month		Day		Year	
Jan	①	⓪	⓪	200	⓪
Feb	②	①	①	200	①
Mar	③	②	②	200	②
Apr	④	③	③	200	③
May	⑤		④	200	④
Jun	⑥		⑤	200	⑤
Jul	⑦		⑥	200	⑥
Aug	⑧		⑦	200	⑦
Sept	⑨		⑧	200	⑧
Oct	⑩		⑨	200	⑨
Nov	⑪				
Dec	⑫				

Test Answers

1. Ⓐ Ⓑ Ⓒ Ⓓ
2. Ⓐ Ⓑ Ⓒ Ⓓ
3. Ⓐ Ⓑ Ⓒ Ⓓ
4. Ⓐ Ⓑ Ⓒ Ⓓ
5. Ⓐ Ⓑ Ⓒ Ⓓ
6. Ⓐ Ⓑ Ⓒ Ⓓ
7. Ⓐ Ⓑ Ⓒ Ⓓ
8. Ⓐ Ⓑ Ⓒ Ⓓ
9. Ⓐ Ⓑ Ⓒ Ⓓ
10. Ⓐ Ⓑ Ⓒ Ⓓ
11. Ⓐ Ⓑ Ⓒ Ⓓ
12. Ⓐ Ⓑ Ⓒ Ⓓ
13. Ⓐ Ⓑ Ⓒ Ⓓ
14. Ⓐ Ⓑ Ⓒ Ⓓ
15. Ⓐ Ⓑ Ⓒ Ⓓ
16. Ⓐ Ⓑ Ⓒ Ⓓ
17. Ⓐ Ⓑ Ⓒ Ⓓ
18. Ⓐ Ⓑ Ⓒ Ⓓ
19. Ⓐ Ⓑ Ⓒ Ⓓ
20. Ⓐ Ⓑ Ⓒ Ⓓ
21. Ⓐ Ⓑ Ⓒ Ⓓ
22. Ⓐ Ⓑ Ⓒ Ⓓ
23. Ⓐ Ⓑ Ⓒ Ⓓ
24. Ⓐ Ⓑ Ⓒ Ⓓ
25. Ⓐ Ⓑ Ⓒ Ⓓ
26. Ⓐ Ⓑ Ⓒ Ⓓ
27. Ⓐ Ⓑ Ⓒ Ⓓ
28. Ⓐ Ⓑ Ⓒ Ⓓ
29. Ⓐ Ⓑ Ⓒ Ⓓ
30. Ⓐ Ⓑ Ⓒ Ⓓ
31. Ⓐ Ⓑ Ⓒ Ⓓ
32. Ⓐ Ⓑ Ⓒ Ⓓ
33. Ⓐ Ⓑ Ⓒ Ⓓ
34. Ⓐ Ⓑ Ⓒ Ⓓ
35. Ⓐ Ⓑ Ⓒ Ⓓ
36. Ⓐ Ⓑ Ⓒ Ⓓ
37. Ⓐ Ⓑ Ⓒ Ⓓ
38. Ⓐ Ⓑ Ⓒ Ⓓ
39. Ⓐ Ⓑ Ⓒ Ⓓ
40. Ⓐ Ⓑ Ⓒ Ⓓ
41. Ⓐ Ⓑ Ⓒ Ⓓ
42. Ⓐ Ⓑ Ⓒ Ⓓ
43. Ⓐ Ⓑ Ⓒ Ⓓ
44. Ⓐ Ⓑ Ⓒ Ⓓ
45. Ⓐ Ⓑ Ⓒ Ⓓ
46. Ⓐ Ⓑ Ⓒ Ⓓ
47. Ⓐ Ⓑ Ⓒ Ⓓ
48. Ⓐ Ⓑ Ⓒ Ⓓ
49. Ⓐ Ⓑ Ⓒ Ⓓ
50. Ⓐ Ⓑ Ⓒ Ⓓ

Stand Out CASAS Style Test Answer Sheet

Student Last Name   First   Middle

Instructor Name

Marking Answers

Use number 2 pencil	Right
Do NOT use pen	(A) (B) ● (D)
Make dark marks that fill out completely	Wrong
Erase completely any answers you change	(A) (⊗) (C) (D) / (A) (B) (C) (⬤)

Student Identification

| (1) (0) (0) (0) (0) (0) (0) (0) (0) |
| (2) (2) (2) (2) (2) (2) (2) (2) (2) |
| (3) (3) (3) (3) (3) (3) (3) (3) (3) |
| (4) (4) (4) (4) (4) (4) (4) (4) (4) |
| (5) (5) (5) (5) (5) (5) (5) (5) (5) |
| (6) (6) (6) (6) (6) (6) (6) (6) (6) |
| (7) (7) (7) (7) (7) (7) (7) (7) (7) |
| (8) (8) (8) (8) (8) (8) (8) (8) (8) |
| (9) (9) (9) (9) (9) (9) (9) (9) (9) |

Test Date

Month	Day	Year
Jan (1)	(0) (0)	200 (0)
Feb (2)	(1) (1)	200 (1)
Mar (3)	(2) (2)	200 (2)
Apr (4)	(3) (3)	200 (3)
May (5)	(4)	200 (4)
Jun (6)	(5)	200 (5)
Jul (7)	(6)	200 (6)
Aug (8)	(7)	200 (7)
Sept (9)	(8)	200 (8)
Oct (10)	(9)	200 (9)
Nov (11)		
Dec (12)		

1 (A) (B) (C) (D)
2 (A) (B) (C) (D)
3 (A) (B) (C) (D)
4 (A) (B) (C) (D)
5 (A) (B) (C) (D)
6 (A) (B) (C) (D)
7 (A) (B) (C) (D)
8 (A) (B) (C) (D)
9 (A) (B) (C) (D)
10 (A) (B) (C) (D)
11 (A) (B) (C) (D)
12 (A) (B) (C) (D)
13 (A) (B) (C) (D)
14 (A) (B) (C) (D)
15 (A) (B) (C) (D)
16 (A) (B) (C) (D)
17 (A) (B) (C) (D)
18 (A) (B) (C) (D)
19 (A) (B) (C) (D)
20 (A) (B) (C) (D)
21 (A) (B) (C) (D)
22 (A) (B) (C) (D)
23 (A) (B) (C) (D)
24 (A) (B) (C) (D)
25 (A) (B) (C) (D)
26 (A) (B) (C) (D)
27 (A) (B) (C) (D)
28 (A) (B) (C) (D)
29 (A) (B) (C) (D)
30 (A) (B) (C) (D)
31 (A) (B) (C) (D)
32 (A) (B) (C) (D)
33 (A) (B) (C) (D)
34 (A) (B) (C) (D)
35 (A) (B) (C) (D)
36 (A) (B) (C) (D)
37 (A) (B) (C) (D)
38 (A) (B) (C) (D)
39 (A) (B) (C) (D)
40 (A) (B) (C) (D)
41 (A) (B) (C) (D)
42 (A) (B) (C) (D)
43 (A) (B) (C) (D)
44 (A) (B) (C) (D)
45 (A) (B) (C) (D)
46 (A) (B) (C) (D)
47 (A) (B) (C) (D)
48 (A) (B) (C) (D)
49 (A) (B) (C) (D)
50 (A) (B) (C) (D)